The only Book of

PARTY PIECES

A COLLECTION OF SONGS, POEMS & AMUSING STORIES

Nuala Harnett

A HARNETT & ROONEY BOOK

First published in Ireland in 2000 by
H & R PUBLISHING
14 Hawkins Street, Dublin 2

Copyright © HARNETT & ROONEY PUBLISHING

All rights reserved. No part of this publication may be produced, stored in a retrieval system, or transmitted in any form or by any means, electronic, mechanical, photocopying, recording or otherwise, without the prior written permission of the copyright owner.

A CIP catalogue record for this book is available from the National Library of Ireland and the British Library.

ISBN: 0-9537609-0-1

Designed and Produced by Rooney Graphics Limited   14 Hawkins Street, Dublin 2
Telephone: + 353 1 679 1943   Facsimile: + 353 1 679 0486   Email: rooneygx@iol.ie   Website: www.rooneygx.com

Printed by Future Print, Grange Way, Baldoyle Industrial Estate, Dublin 13.
Telephone: + 353 1 839 2070   Facsimile: + 353 1 839 2591

Foreword by Terry Wogan

*T*he bit of "craic" is one of Ireland's noblest traditions. Wherever there's a party, there'll be songs and stories. However, not all of us have a song in our hearts, nor a story on our lips at the drop of a hat - and it can be very embarrassing when **your** turn comes - to come to the aid of the party - to stand there - mumchance, without a thought in your head.

And this, my fellow-revellers, is where Nuala's invaluable little tome comes in. You need never be stuck for a bar of a song, or a bit of the airy banter, ever again.

I can see you now, the life and soul of the party! You'd better employ a social secretary - your life's never going to be the same again.

Terry Wogan

Introduction

*E*veryone enjoys a good party or get-together where there is a warm friendly atmosphere. The most memorable occasions are often when the party guests entertain themselves. One person can start the ball rolling by singing a song, everyone gathers around, and one by one others make a contribution. I experienced these evenings as a child at home around the fire, and later while visiting Achill Island off the West Coast of Ireland. If you could perform a Party Piece you were welcome everywhere.

Most people feel they would like to do something, but "don't know the words". Now, you too can amuse and entertain your friends by learning your own Party Piece. Here is a selection of well-known songs, interesting poems and amusing stories for you to choose from.

If you can sing there is a **song** that suits you. You already know the tune, now you have the words.

If you don't wish to sing, recite a **poem**. There are some for the accomplished performer, and others that are amusing or emotionally stirring that anyone can say.

If you are not good at remembering your lines it it easier to tell an **amusing story**. If it amuses you, tell it in your own way and everyone will enjoy it.

Join in and make a good party great.

Nuala Harnett

Contents

SONGS

Annie's Song	10
Unforgettable	10
When I Fall in Love	10
It's a Long Way to Tipperary	10
Lady in Red	11
When Irish Eyes Are Smiling	11
As Time Goes By	12
Danny Boy	12
Cockles and Mussels	13
Strangers In The Night	13
My Way	15
Something Stupid	16
I'll Take you home again Kathleen	16
Galway Bay	17
All My Loving	17
Wild Rover	18
Wild Mountain Thyme	18
Summertime	19
Tonight	19
Yesterday	19
Edelweiss	19
When I'm Sixty-Four	21
Hey Jude	22
O What A Beautiful Morning	23
Wouldn't It be Loverly	23
Memory	25
Morning Has Broken	26
Jamaica Farewell	26
Ol' Man River	27
King of the Road	28
Scarborough Fair	28
Sounds of Silence	29
You'll Never Walk Alone	29
Blowin' In the Wind	31
Sweet Caroline	31
Rock around the Clock	32
I Can't Help Falling In Love With You	32
Raindrops Keep Falling On My Head	33
Big Spender	33
Those Were the Days	34
Downtown	35
White Christmas	35
I Just Called to Say I Love You	36
Love & Marriage	36
He'll Have to Go	37
House of the Rising Sun	37
Nora	38
When the Saints Go Marching In	38
Somewhere	39
The Light Of Other Days	39
The Meeting Of The Waters	40
Send In The Clowns	41
Unchained Melody	41
It's Now Or Never	42
Somewhere My Love	42
The Fields of Athenry	43
We'll meet again	43

POEMS

My Neighbour's Roses	46
A Flea and a Fly	46
My neighbour's Reply	46
One Little Boy	47
Another Little Boy	47
Evolution	48
He Wishes for the Cloths of Heaven	48
The People Upstairs	48
Golf is	49
I'm The Dog Who Didn't Win A Prize	50
My Time of Day	51
Hugs	51

Visit the Sick	52
Adipose Auntie's Pose	52
A Piper	52
Leisure	53
The Daffodils	53
George The Giraffe	55
Your Neighbour	55
The Lake Isle of Innisfree	56
Down by the Salley Gardens	56
An Old Woman of the Roads	57
The Way we Tell a Story	57
"If I was a Lady"	58
The Horse's Farewell to His Cowboy	59
Mary - the lamb and the bear	60
The Poem	60
Erasers	60
Oh, I wish I'd looked after me Teeth	61
Ach, I Dunno!	63
Lil of Kilquade	63
If	64
A Pint of Plain is your Only Man	65
Tell Him Now	65
A Noble Boy	66
The Pig	67
Indispensable	67
Around the Corner	68
On a Tired Housewife	68
Work	68
Christmas Greetings	69
Poor Beasts	71
Lay not up	71
First Parting	72
Please Call	72
Together	73
Chains	73
Middle Age	74
Jim	74
Desiderata	75
If I Had My Life To Live Over	76
An Irish Toast	77
An Irish Toast	77
Looking the Part	77
My Son the Bridegroom	78
Spring in the Bronx	78
Castaway	78
The English Language	79

AMUSING STORIES

Big Chief Forget-me-Not	82
Mummy's Tummy	82
First Aid Course	83
Eton Schoolboys	83
Hair-cut	83
Hen-Pecked Husband	84
Honey, If I Died	84
Pirate's Story	85
House Builder	85
Phone-call	85
Old Man Dying	87
Cats In Heaven	87
Baby Priscilla	87
Winnie the Pooh	88
The Artist	88
Memento	88
We Survived!	89
Golf Lesson	91
Banker In Love	91
The beggar	91
Going To A Party	92
George Bernard Shaw	92
Las Vegas	92
In a Foreign Land	93
Doctor's Reception	93
The Fight	93
Rodeo Champion	95
New Route for Train	95
Doctor/Patient	95
Visiting The Pope	96
Two Irish Astronauts	96

Songs

In this section there is a wide variety of songs to choose from - Irish ballads, hits from musicals and classic favourites.

If you are a competent singer and don't go off key, pick a song with lots of melody. Learn the words well and, when performing it, stand, hold your head up and sing out.

If you have an average voice, choose a catchy song with a good beat and not too wide a range. Smile at your audience and encourage them to join in the chorus.

Annie's Song
John Denver

You fill up my senses like a night in the forest
Like the mountains in springtime,
Like a walk in the rain
Like a storm in the desert,
Like a sleepy blue ocean
You fill up my senses, come fill me again.

Come let me love you,
let me give my love to you
Let me drown in your laughter,
Let me die in your arms
Let me lay down beside you,
Let me always be with you
Come let me love you, come love me again.

Unforgettable
Irving Gordon

Unforgettable, that's what you are
Unforgettable, tho' near or far
Like a song of love that clings to me
How the thought of you does things to me
Never before has someone been more
Unforgettable in ev'ry way
And for evermore, that's how you'll stay
That's why Darling, it's incredible
That someone so unforgettable
Thinks that I am unforgettable too.

When I Fall in Love
Edward Heyman/Victor Young

When I fall in love it will be forever
or I'll never fall in love.
In a restless world like this is,
love is ended before it's begun,
And too many moonlight kisses
seem to cool in the warmth of the sun.

When I give my heart it will be completely
or I'll never give my heart.
And the moment I can feel that
you feel that way too,
Is when I fall in love with you

It's a Long Way to Tipperary
Judge/Williams

Its a long way to Tipperary,
it's a long way to go
Its a long way to Tipperary
to the sweetest girl I know!
Goodbye, Piccadilly,
Farewell Leicester Square
Its a long, long way to Tipperary,
but my heart's right there!

PARTY PIECES   SONGS

Lady in Red
Chris De Burgh

I've never seen you looking so lovely as you did tonight
I've never seen you shine so bright mm mm mm mm
I've never seen so many men ask you if you wanted to dance
They're looking for a little romance, given half a chance
And I've never seen that dress you're wearing
Or the highlights in your hair that catch your eyes
I have been blind.

The lady in red is dancing with me, cheek to cheek
There's nobody here, its just you and me
It's where I want to be
But I hardly know this beauty by my side
I'll never forget the way you look tonight.

I've never seen you looking so gorgeous as you did to-night,
I've never seen so many people want to be there by your side,
And when you turned to me and smiled it took my breath away
And I've never had such a feeling of complete and utter love as I did tonight.

When Irish Eyes Are Smiling
Olcott/Graff/Ball

When Irish eyes are smiling,
Sure it's like a morn in spring
In the lilt of Irish laughter
You can hear the angels sing
When Irish hearts are happy,
All the world seems bright & gay
And when Irish eyes are smiling
Sure they steal your heart away.

11

Party Pieces

Songs

As Time Goes By
Words and music by Herman Hupfield

You must remember this,
A kiss is still a kiss,
A sigh is just a sigh
The fundamental things apply,
As time goes by.
And when two lovers woo, they still say,
"I love you", On that you can rely;
No matter what the future brings,
As time goes by.

Moonlight and love songs never out of date,
Hearts full of passion, jealousy and hate;
Woman needs man and man must have his mate,
That no one can deny.

It's still the same old story,
A fight for love and glory.
A case of do or die!
The world will always welcome lovers,
As time goes by.

Danny Boy
Weatherly

O Danny Boy, the pipes, the pipes are calling
From glen to glen & down the mountain side
The summer's gone & all the flowers are dying
'Tis you, 'tis you must go & I must bide.
But come you back when summer's in the meadow
Or when the valley's hushed & white with snow
'Tis I'll be there in sunshine or in shadow
O Danny Boy, O Danny Boy, I love you so.

And when you come and all the flowers are dying
And if I'm dead, as dead I well may be
You'll come & find the place where I am lying
And kneel & say an "Ave" there for me.

And I shall hear, tho' soft you tread above me
And all my dreams will warm & sweeter be
If you will bend and tell me that you love me
Then I shall sleep in peace until you come to me.

PARTY PIECES   SONGS

Cockles and Mussels
Trad.

In Dublin's fair city where the girls are so pretty
I first set my eyes on sweet Molly Malone
She wheeled her wheelbarrow through
streets broad & narrow
Crying "cockles & mussels alive alive-0!"
Alive alive-o, alive alive o
Crying "cockles & mussels alive alive-o!"

She was a fishmonger but sure 'twas no wonder
For so were her father & mother before
And they both wheeled their barrow
through streets broad & narrow
Crying "cockles & mussels alive alive-0!"
Alive alive-o, alive alive o
Crying "cockles & mussels alive alive-o!"

She died of a fever & no one could save her
And that was the end of sweet Molly Malone
Now her ghost wheels her barrow
through streets broad & narrow
Crying "cockles & mussels alive alive-0!"
Alive alive-o, alive alive o
Crying "cockles & mussels alive alive-o!"

Strangers In The Night
Singleton/Snyder/Kaempfert

Strangers in the night exchanging glances
Wond'ring in the night
What were the chances we'd be sharing love
Before the night was through.

Something in your eyes was so inviting
Something in your smile was so exciting,
Something in my heart,
Told me I must have you.

Strangers in the night, two lonely people
We were strangers in the night
Up to the moment
When we said our first hello.
Little did we know
Love was just a glance away,
A warm embracing dance away and -

Ever since that night we've been together
Lovers at first sight, in love forever,
It turned out so right,
For strangers in the night.

My Way
Revaux/Francois/Anka

And now the end is near
And so I face the final curtain.
My friend, I'll say it clear,
I'll state my case, of which I'm certain.
I've lived a life that's full.
I've travelled each and ev'ry highway;
But more, much more than this,
I did it my way.

Regrets, I've had a few
But then again, too few to mention.
I did what I had to do
And saw it through without exemption.
I planned each charted course;
Each careful step along the byway,
But more, much more than this,
I did it my way.

Yes, there were times, I'm sure you knew
When I bit off more than I could chew.
But through it all, when there was doubt,
I ate it up and spit it out,
I faced it all and I stood tall;
And did it my way.

I've loved, I've laughed and cried.
I've had my fill, my share of losing,
And now, as tears subside,
I find it all so amusing
To think I did all that
And may I say - not in a shy way,
"Oh no, oh no not me,
I did it my way:"

For what is a man, what has he got?
If not himself, then he has naught
To say the things he truly feels
And not the words of one who kneels.
The record shows I took the blows -
And did it my way!

Something Stupid
Parks

I know I stand in line until you think you have the time
To spend an evening with me
And if we go someplace to dance,
I know that there's a chance
You won't be leaving with me.

And afterwards we drop into a quiet little place
And have a drink or two
And then I go and spoil it all by
saying something stupid
Like: "I love you".

I can see it in your eyes,
that you despise the same old lies
You heard the night before
And though it's just a line to you, for me it's true
And never seemed so right before.

I practice every day to find some clever lines to say
To make the meaning come through
But then I think I'll wait until the evening gets late
And I'm alone with you.

The time is right your perfume fills my head,
the stars get red
And oh the night's so blue
And then I go and spoil it all,
By saying something stupid
Like: "I love you"
("I love you, I love you, ...")

I'll Take You Home Again Kathleen
Westendorf

I'll take you home again Kathleen
Across the ocean wild and wide
To where your heart has ever been
Since first you were my bonny bride
The roses all have left your cheeks
I've watched them fade away and die
Your voice is sad whene'er you speak
And tears be dim your loving eyes

Refrain

Oh, I will take you back Kathleen
To where your heart will feel no pain,
And when the fields are fresh and green
I will take you to your home Kathleen

I know you love me, Kathleen dear,
Your heart was ever fond and true;
I always feel when you are near
That life holds nothing dear but you
The smiles that once you gave to me
I scarcely ever see them now
Tho' many many times I see
The darkening shadows on your brow.

Refrain

PARTY PIECES   SONGS

Galway Bay
Calahan

If you ever go across the sea to Ireland,
Then may it be at the closing of your day
You will sit and watch the moon rise over Claddagh
And see the sun go down on Galway Bay.

Just to hear again the ripple of the trout stream
The women in the meadows making hay
And to sit beside a turf fire in the cabin
And watch the barefoot gossoons at their play.

For the breezes blowing o'er the seas from Ireland
Are perfumed by the heather as they blow
And the women in the uplands digging praties
Speak a language that the strangers do not know.

For the strangers came and tried to teach us their way.
They scorned us just for being what we are
But they might as well go chasing after moon beams
Or light a penny candle from a star.

And if there's going to be a life here after
And somehow I am sure there's going to be,
I will ask my God to let me make my heaven
In that dear land across the Irish Sea.

All My Loving
The Beatles

Close your eyes and I'll kiss you,
Tomorrow I'll miss you;
Remember I'll always be true.
And then while I'm away,
I'll write home ev'ry day
And I'll send all my loving to you.

I'll pretend that I'm kissing
The lips I am missing
And hope that my dreams will come true
And then while I'm away,
I'll write home ev'ry day,
And I'll send all my loving to you.

All my loving I will send to you.
All my loving, darling I'll be true.

17

Wild Rover
Trad.

I've been a wild rover for many a year
And I've spent all my money on whiskey & beer
But now I'm returning with gold in great store
And I never will play the wild rover no more

Chorus
And it's no, nay, never No, nay never no more
Will I play the wild rover No never, no more.

I went into an alehouse I used to frequent
I told the landlady my money was spent
I asked her for credit she answered me "Nay
Such custom as yours I can have any day"

Chorus

I took out from my pocket ten sovereigns bright
And the landlady's eyes opened wide with delight
She said "I've got whiskeys & wines of the best
And the words that I spoke they were only in jest"

Chorus

I'll go home to my parents confess what I've done
And I'll ask them to pardon their prodigal son
And if they forgive me, as oft times before
Sure I never will play the wild rover no more.

Wild Mountain Thyme
Trad.

O, the summertime is coming
And the trees are sweetly blooming,
And the wild mountain thyme,
Grows around the purple heather
Will you go, lassie go

Chorus
And we'll all go together
To pluck wild mountain thyme,
All around the blooming heather
Will you go, Lassie go?

I will build my love a tower
Near yon pure crystal fountain,
And round it I will place,
All the flowers of the mountain,
Will you go, lassie, go?

Chorus

If my true love she were gone,
I would surely find another,
Where wild mountain thyme,
Grows around the blooming heather,
Will you go, lassie, go?

Chorus

Party Pieces — Songs

Summertime
Heyward/Gershwin

Summertime & the livin' is easy
Fish are jumpin' & the cotton is high
O your pappy's rich & your mammy's good lookin'
So hush little baby don't you cry.

One of these mornings you're gonna rise up singin'
Then you'll spread your wings & you'll take to the sky
Until that mornin' there ain't nothin' can harm you
with mammy & pappy standin' by.

Tonight
Sondheim/Bernstein

Tonight, tonight, won't be just any night
Tonight there will be no morning star
Tonight, tonight, I'll see my love tonight
And for us stars will stop where they are.

Today the minutes seem like hours,
The hours go so slowly
And still the sky is light
O moon grow bright & make this endless day
Endless night, tonight

Yesterday
Lennon/McCartney

Yesterday, all my troubles seemed so far away
Now it looks as though they're here to stay
Oh, I believe in yesterday.

Suddenly, I'm not half the man I used to be,
There's a shadow hanging over me
Oh, yesterday came suddenly.

Why she had to go I don't know she wouldn't say.
I said something wrong, now I long for yesterday.

Yesterday, love was such an easy game to play.
Now I need a place to hide away.
Oh, I believe in yesterday.

Edelweiss
Hammerstein/Rodgers

Edelweiss, Edelweiss
Every morning you greet me
Small & white, clean & bright
You look happy to meet me
Blossoms of snow may you bloom & grow
Bloom & grow forever
Edelweiss, Edelweiss,
Bless my homeland forever

When I'm Sixty-Four
Lennon/McCartney

When I get older, losing my hair
Many years from now
Will you still be sending me a Valentine,
Birthday greetings, bottle of wine.

If I've been out till quarter to three
Would you lock the door
Will you still need me, will you still feed me
When I'm sixty- four.

You'll be older too,
And if you say the word I could stay with you.

I could be handy mending a fuse
When your lights have gone
You can knit a sweater by the fireside
Sunday mornings go for a ride

Doing the garden, digging the weeds,
Who could ask for more
Will you still need me, will you still feed me
When I'm sixty- four.

Every summer we can rent a cottage
in the Isle of Wight,
If it's not too dear
We shall scrimp and save
Grandchildren on your knee,
Vera, Chuck & Dave.

Send me a postcard, drop me a line
Stating point of view
Indicate precisely, what you mean to say
Yours sincerely, wasting away.

Give me your answer, fill in a form,
Mine for evermore
Will you still need me, will you still feed me
When I'm sixty-four.

Party Pieces — Songs

Hey Jude
Lennon/McCartney

Hey Jude, don't make it bad,
Take a sad song and make it better,
Remember to let her into your heart,
Then you can start to make it better.

Hey Jude, don't be afraid.
You were made to go out and get her.
The minute you let her under your skin,
Then you begin to make it better.

And anytime you feel the pain, hey Jude, refrain,
Don't carry the world upon your shoulder.
For well you know that it's a fool who plays it cool
By making his world a little colder.

Na na na na na na

Hey Jude, don't let me down.
You have found her, now go and get her.
Remember to let her into your heart,
Then you can start to make it better.

So let it out and let it in, hey Jude begin,
You're waiting for someone to perform with.
And don't you know that it's just you,
Hey Jude, you'll do,
The movement you need is on your shoulder.
Na na na na na na …

Hey Jude, don't make it bad.
Take a sad song and make it better.
Remember to let her under your skin
Then you'll begin to make it
Better better better better better better, oh.

Na na na, na na na, na na na na
hey Jude …

PARTY PIECES  SONGS

O What A Beautiful Morning
Rodgers and Hammerstein

There's a bright golden haze on the meadow
There's a bright golden haze on the meadow
The corn is as high as an elephant's eye
And it looks like its climbing right up to the sky.

Chorus
O what a beautiful morning,
O what a beautiful day
I've got a beautiful feeling,
Everything's going my way.

All the cattle are standing like statues
All the cattle are standing like statues
They don't turn their heads as they see me ride by
But a little brown mav'rick is winking her eye.

Chorus

All the sounds of the earth are like music
All the sounds of the earth are like music
The breeze is so busy it don't miss a tree
And an ol' weeping willow is laughing at me

Chorus

Wouldn't It be Loverly
Lerner/Loewe

All I want is a room somewhere
Far away from the cold night air
With one enormous chair
O wouldn't it be loverly?

Lots of choc'late for me to eat
Lots of coal makin' lots of heat
Warm face, warm hands, warm feet
O wouldn't it be loverly?

O, so loverly sittin' abso-bloomin-lutely still
I would never budge til spring
Crept over me winder sill.

Someone's head restin' on my knee
Warm & tender as he can be
Who takes good care of me
O wouldn't it be loverly,
loverly, loverly loverly loverly.

Memory
Andrew Lloyd Webber

Memory, not a sound from the pavement.
Has the moon lost her memory?
She is smiling alone.
In the lamp light the withered leaves
collect at my feet
And the wind begins to moan.

Mem'ry all alone in the moonlight
I can smile at the old days
I was beautiful then
I remember the time I knew what happiness was
Let the mem'ry live again.

Ev'ry street lamp seems to beat
A fatalistic warning
Someone mutters and a street lamp gutters
And soon it will be morning.

Daylight I must wait for the sunrise
I must think of a new life
And I musn't give in
When the dawn comes
Tonight will be a memory too
And a new day will begin.

Burnt out ends of smoky days
The stale cold smell of morning
The street lamp dies another night is over
Another day is dawning.

Touch me
It's so easy to leave me
All alone with the memory
Of my days in the sun
If you touch me you'll understand what happiness is
Look a new day has begun.

Morning Has Broken
Farjean/Trad.

Morning has broken like the first morning
Blackbird has spoken like the first bird
Praise for the singing, praise for the morning
Praise for the springing fresh from the Word.

Sweet the rain's new fall sunlit from heaven
Like the first dew fall on the first grass
Praise for the sweetness of the wet garden
Sprung in completeness where His feet pass.

Mine is the sunlight, mine is the morning
Born of the one light Eden saw play
Praise with elation, praise every morning
God's re-creation of the new day

Jamaica Farewell
Irving Burgie

Down the way where the nights are gay
And the sun shines brightly on the mountain top
I took a trip on a sailing ship
And when I reached Jamaica I made a stop.

Chorus
But I am sad to say I'm on my way
Won't be back for many a day
My heart is down, my head is turning around
Had to leave a little girl in Kingston town.

Sound of laughter everywhere
And the dancers swinging to & fro
I must declare that my heart is there
Tho' I've been from Maine to Mexico.

Chorus

Down at the market you can hear
Ladies cry out while on their heads they bear
Ake rice, salt fish are nice
And the rum is fine anytime of year.

Chorus

Ol' Man River
Hammerstein/Kern

Here we all work 'long the Mississippi
Here we all work while the white folk play
Pullin' them boats from the dawn till sunset
Gettin' no rest till the judgment day.

Don't look up and don't look down
You don't das make the boss man frown
Bend your knees and bow your head
And pull that rope until your dead

Let me go 'way from the Mississippi
Let me go 'way from the white man boss
Show me that stream called the River Jordan
That's the old stream that I long to cross.

Ol' Man River that Ol' Man River
He don't say nothing,
But he must know somethin'
He just keeps rollin'
He just keeps rollin along.

He don't plant tatters, and he don't plant cotton
And them what plants em, are soon forgotten
But Ol' Man River, just keeps rollin' along.

You and me we sweat and strain
Body all achin' and racked with pain
Tote that barge and lift that bail
You get a little drunk and you lands in jail.

I gets weary and sick of trying
I'm tired of living, but I'm scared of dyin'
But Ol' Man River, he just keeps rollin' along.

PARTY PIECES 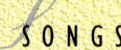SONGS

King of the Road
Roger Miller

Trailer for sale or rent - rooms to let: 50 cents
No phone, no pool, no pets
I ain't got no cigarettes
Ah but, two hours of pushing broom
Buys an 8 by 12 four-bit room.
I'm a man of means by no means,
King of the Road.

Third boxcar, midnight train
Destination: Bangor, Maine
Old worn out suit & shoes. I don't pay no union dues
I smoke old stogies I have found,
Short but not too big around
I'm a man of means by no means
King of the Road.

I know every engineer on every train
All of the children & all of their names
And every handout in every town
And ev'ry lock that ain't locked when no one's around.
Trailer for sale or rent ...

Scarborough Fair
Trad.

Are you going to Scarborough Fair?
Parsley, sage, rosemary & thyme
Remember me to one who lives there
For she once was a true love of mine.

Tell her to make me a cambric shirt,
Parsley, sage, rosemary & thyme
Without any seam or fine needlework
And then she'll be a true love of mine

Tell her to find me an acre of land
Parsley, sage, rosemary and thyme
Between the salt waters and the sea strand
Then she'll be a true love of mine.

Tell her to reap it with a sickle of leather,
Parsley, sage, rosemary and thyme
And gather it all in a bunch of heather
Then she'll be a true love of mine.

And when you have done & finished your work
Parsley, sage, rosemary and thyme
Then come to me for your cambric shirt
Then you'll be a true love of mine.

PARTY PIECES   SONGS

Sounds of Silence
Paul Simon

Hello darkness my old friend
I've come to talk to you again
Because a vision softly creeping
Left its seeds while I was sleeping
And the vision that was planted in my brain
Still remains - within the sounds of silence.

In restless dreams I walked alone
Narrow streets of cobblestone
'Neath the halo of a street lamp
I turned my collar to the cold & damp
When my eyes were stabbed by the flash of a neon light
That split the night - & touched the sound of silence.

And in the naked light I saw
10,000 people, maybe more.
People talking without speaking
People hearing without listening
People writing songs that voices never shared
No one dared, disturb the sound of silence.

"Fools" said I "You do not know
Silence like a cancer grows
Hear my words that I might teach you
Take my arms that I might reach you"
But my words like silent raindrops fell(pause)
And echoed in the well of silence.

And the people bowed and prayed
To the neon god they'd made
And the sign flashed out its warning
In the words that it was forming
And the sign said "The words of the prophets are written on subway walls
And tenement halls -
And whisper in the sounds of silence"

You'll Never Walk Alone
Rodgers & Hammerstein

When you walk through a storm
Hold your head up high
And don't be afraid of the dark.
At the end of the storm is a golden sky
And the sweet silver song of the lark.
Walk on through the wind,
Walk on through the rain,
Tho' your dreams be tossed and blown.
Walk on, walk on with hope in your heart
And you'll never Walk Alone,
You'll never Walk Alone.

Party Pieces — Songs

SONGS

Blowin' In the Wind
Bob Dylan

How many roads must a man walk down
Before you call him a man?
Yes & how many seas must a white dove sail
Before she sleeps in the sand?
Yes & how many times must the cannonballs fly
Before they're forever banned?
The answer, my friend, is blowin' in the wind
The answer is blowin' in the wind.

How many times must a man look up
Before he can see the sky?
Yes & how many ears must one man have
Before he can hear people cry?
Yes & how many deaths will it take till he knows
That too many people have died?
The answer, my friend, is blowin' in the wind
The answer is blowin' in the wind

How many years can a mountain exist
Before it's washed to the sea?
Yes & how many years can some people exist
Before they're allowed to be free?
Yes & how many times can a man turn his head
Pretending he just doesn't see?
The answer, my friend, is blowin' in the wind
The answer is blowin' in the wind

Sweet Caroline
Neil Diamond

Where it began, I can't begin to knowing
But then I know it's growing strong
Was in the spring
Then spring became the summer
Who'd have believed you'd come along

Hands touching hands
Reaching out, touching me, touching you

Sweet Caroline
Good times never seemed so good
I'd been inclined
To believe they never would
So good, so good.

Look at the night and it don't seem so lonely
We fill it up with only two
And when I hurt
Hurting runs off my shoulder
How can I hurt when I'm holding you

Warm touching warm,
Reaching out, touching me, touching you

Sweet Caroline
Good times never seemed so good
I'd been inclined
To believe they never would
Sweet Caroline

PARTY PIECES   SONGS

Rock around the Clock
Freedman/de Knight

One, two, three o'clock, four o'clock rock,
Five, six, seven o'clock, eight o'clock rock,
Nine, ten, eleven o'clock, twelve o'clock rock,
We're gonna rock around the clock tonight.

Put your glad rags on and join me, Hon,
We'll have some fun when the clock strikes one

Chorus
We're gonna rock around the clock tonight,
We're gonna rock, rock, rock, 'till broad day light,
We're gonna rock, gonna rock around the clock tonight.

When the clock strikes two, and three and four,
If the band slows down we'll yell for more,
We're gonna rock ... *Chorus*

When the chimes ring five and six and seven
We'll be rockin' up in seventh heaven,
We're gonna rock ... *Chorus*

When it's eight, nine, ten, eleven, too,
I'll be goin' strong and so will you
We're gonna rock ... *Chorus*

When the clock strikes twelve, we'll cool off then,
Start a rockin' 'round the clock again
We're gonna rock ... *Chorus*

I Can't Help Falling In Love With You

Wise men say only fools rush in,
But I can't help falling in love with you.

Shall I stay, would it be a sin,
If I can't help falling in love with you.

Like a river flows surely to the sea
Darling so it goes, some things are meant to be.

Take my hand, take my whole life too
For I can't help falling in love with you.

PARTY PIECES   SONGS

Raindrops Keep Falling On My Head
Burt Bacharach

Raindrops keep falling on my head
And just like the guy whose feet are
too big for his bed
Nothin' seems to fit
Those raindrops are falling on
my head they keep falling.

So I just did me some talkin' to the sun
And I said I didn't like the way
he got things done
Sleepin' on the job
Those raindrops are falling on
my head they keep falling.

But there's one thing I know
The blues he sends to meet me
won't defeat me
It won't be long till happiness steps
up to greet me.

Raindrops keep falling on my head
But that doesn't mean my eyes will
soon be turnin' red
Crying's not for me
Cause I'm never gonna stop the rain by complainin'
Because I'm free
Nothing's worrying me.

Big Spender
Fields/Coleman

The minute you walked in the joint
I could see you were a man of distinction
A real big spender, good looking, so refined
Say, wouldn't you like to know what's
going on in my mind
So let me get right to the point
I don't pop my cork for every guy I see
Hey! big Spender, spend a little time with me.

Wouldn't you like to have fun, fun, fun?
How's about a few laughs, laughs?
I can show you a good time
Let me show you a good time

The minute you walked in the joint
I could see you were a man of distinction
A real big spender, good looking, so refined
Say, wouldn't you like to know what's
going on in my mind
So let me get right to the point
I don't pop my cork for every guy I see

Hey Big Spender, Hey Big Spender,
Spend a little time with me
Spend a little time with me
Spend a little time with me.

Those Were the Days
Gene Raskin

Once upon a time there was a tavern
Where we used to raise a glass or two
Remember how we laughed away the hours
And dreamed of all the great things we would do

Chorus
Those were the days my friend,
We thought they'd never end
We'd sing & dance forever & a day
We'd live the life we choose,
We'd fight & never lose
For we were young & sure to have our way
La, la, la ...
Those were they days, O yes, those were the days

Then the busy years went rushing by us
We lost our starry notions on the way
If by chance I'd see you in the tavern
We'd smile at one another & we'd say:

Chorus ... those were the days ...

Just tonight I stood before the tavern
Nothing seemed the way it used to be
In the glass I saw a strange reflection
Was that lonely person really me?

Chorus ... those were the days ...

Thru the door there came familiar laughter
I saw your face & heard you call my name
O my friends, we're older but no wiser
For in our hearts the dreams are
still the same!

Chorus ... those were the days ...

Downtown
Tony Hatch

When you're alone & life is making you lonely
You can always go - downtown
When you've got worries all the noise & the hurry
Seem to help I know - downtown
Linger on the sidewalks where
the neon signs are pretty
Listen to the music of the traffic in the city
How can you lose?

Chorus
The lights are much brighter there
You can forget all your troubles
Forget all your cares
And go downtown where all the lights are bright
Downtown - waiting for you tonight
Downtown - its gonna be all right now.

Don't hang around and let your
troubles surround you
There are movie shows - downtown
Maybe you know some little places to go to
Where they never close - downtown
Listen to the rhythm of a gentle bossa nova
You'll be dancing with it too before
the night is over
Happy again

Chorus

White Christmas
Words & music by Irving Berlin

I'm dreaming of a white Christmas,
Just like the ones I used to know,
Where those tree-tops glisten
And children listen
To hear sleighbells in the snow.

I'm dreaming of a white Christmas,
With every Christmas card I write,
"May your days be merry and bright,
And may all your Christmases be white"

I'm dreaming of a white Christmas,
Just like the ones I used to know.
May your days be merry and bright,
And may all your Christmases be white

I Just Called to Say I Love You
Stevie Wonder

No New Years Day to celebrate
No chocolate covered candy hearts to give away
No first of spring, no song to sing
In fact here's just another ordinary day

Chorus
I just called to say I love you
I just called to say how much I care
I just called to say I love you
And I mean it from the bottom of my heart

No April rain, no flowers' bloom
No wedding Saturday within the month of June
But what it is, is something true
Made up of these three words that
I must say to you

Chorus

No summer's high, no warm July
No harvest moon to light one tender August night
No autumn breeze, no falling leaves
Not even time for birds to fly to southern skies.

Chorus

No Libra sun, no Halloween
No giving thanks to all the Christmas joy you bring
But what it is, tho' old so new
To fill your heart like no three words could ever do

Chorus

Love & Marriage
Cahn/Van Heusen

Love and marriage, Love and marriage,
Go together like a horse and carriage
This I tell you brother,
You can't tell one without the other.

Love and marriage, love and marriage
It's an institute you can't disparage,
Ask the local gentry
And they will say it's elementary.

Try, try, try to separate them,
It's an illusion,
Try, try, try and you will only come
To this conclusion.

Love and marriage, love and marriage
Go together like a horse and carriage
Dad was told by mother
You can't have one, you can't have none
You can't have one without the other.

He'll Have to Go
Allison/Allison

Put your sweet lips a little closer to the phone
Let's pretend that we're together all alone.
I'll tell the man to turn the juke box way down low
And you can tell your friend there with you he'll have to go.

Whisper to me, tell me do you love me true?
Or is he holding you the way I do
Tho' love is blind, make up your mind, I've got to know
Should I hang up or will you tell him - he'll have to go

You can't say the words I want to hear
while you're with another man
If you want me to answer "yes" or "no"
Darling I will understand

Put your sweet lips a little closer to the phone
Let's pretend that we're together all alone.
I'll tell the man to turn the juke box way down low
And you can tell your friend there with you he'll have to go.

House of the Rising Sun
Lomax/Turner

There is a house in New Orleans,
They call the Rising Sun
It's been the ruin of many a poor girl
And me, O Lord, I'm one

If I'd listened to what Mama said,
I'd a been at home today
But I was young and foolish, poor girl,
Let a gambler lead me astray.

Go tell my baby sister, don't do like I have done
To shun that house in New Orleans,
They call the Rising Sun.

I'm going back to New Orleans,
My race is almost run
Going back to spend the rest of my life
Beneath that Rising Sun.

Nora
Trad.

The violets were scenting the woods, Nora,
Displaying their charms to the bees,
When I first said I loved only you, Nora,
And you said you loved only me.

The chestnuts' bloom beams through the glade, Nora,
The robins sang from every tree.
When I first said I loved only you Nora,
And you said you loved only me.

The golden dewed daffodils shone, Nora
And danced in the breeze on the lea,
When I first said I loved only you, Nora,
And you said you loved only me.

The birds in the trees sang their songs, Nora
Of happier transports to be
When I first said I loved only you, Nora,
And you said you loved only me.

Our hopes they have never come true, Nora,
Our dreams they were never to be
Since I first said I loved only you, Nora
And you said you loved only me.

The violets are withered and gone, Nora,
I cry for the years as they flee,
Since I first said I loved only you, Nora,
And you said you loved only me.

When the Saints Go Marching In

O when the saints go marching in
O when the saints go marching in
I want to be in that number
When the saints go marching in.

And when the sun begins to shine
And when the sun begins to shine
I want to be in that number
When the sun begins to shine.

O when the trumpet sounds the call
O when the trumpet sounds the call
I want to be in that number
When the trumpet sounds the call.

O when the saints go marching in, etc ...

Somewhere
Bernstein/Sondheim
From West Side Story

There's a place for us,
Somewhere a place for us
Peace and quiet and open air
Wait for us, somewhere.

There's a time for us,
Some day a time for us,
Time together with time to spare,
Time to learn, time to care,
Some-day, some-where.

We'll find a new way of living
We'll find a way of forgiving,
Some-where ...

There's a place for us,
A time and place for us.
Hold my hand and we're half way there,
Hold my hand and I'll take you there
Some-how, Some-day, Some-where.

The Light Of Other Days
T. Moore

Oft in the stilly night
Ere slumber's chain has bound me,
Fond Memory brings the light
Of other days around me:
The smiles, the tears
Of boyhood's years,
The words of love then spoken;
The eyes that shone,
Now dimm'd and gone,
The cheerful hearts now broken!
Thus in the stilly night
Ere slumber's chain has bound me,
Sad Memory brings the light
Of other days around me.

When I remember all
The friends so link'd together
I've seen around me fall
Like leaves in wintry weather,
I feel like one
Who treads alone
Some banquet-hall deserted,
Whose lights are fled
Whose garlands dead,
And all but he departed!

Thus in the stilly night
Ere slumber's chain has bound me,
Sad Memory brings the light
Of other days around me.

PARTY PIECES   SONGS

The Meeting Of The Waters
Thomas Moore

There is not in the wide world a valley so sweet
As that vale in whose bosom the bright waters meet;
Oh! the last rays of feeling and life must depart,
Ere the bloom of that valley shall fade from my heart.

Yet it *was* not that Nature had shed o'er the scene
Her purest of crystal and brightest of green;
'Twas *not* her soft magic of streamlet or hill,
Oh! no - it was something more exquisite still.

'Twas that friends, the belov'd of my bosom, were near,
Who made every dear scene of enchantment more dear,
And who felt how the best charms of nature improve,
When we see them reflected from looks that we love.

Sweet vale of Avoca! how calm could I rest
In thy bosom of shade, with the friends I love best,
Where the storms that we feel in this cold world should cease,
And our hearts, like thy waters, be mingled in peace.

PARTY PIECES · SONGS

Send In The Clowns
Stephen Sondheim

Isn't it rich? Aren't we a pair?
Me here at last on the ground,
you in mid air
Send in the clowns

Isn't it bliss? Don't you approve?
One who keeps tearing around,
one who can't move
Where are the clowns?
Send in the clowns

Just when I'd stopped opening doors
Finally knowing the one that I wanted was yours
Making my entrance again with my usual flair
Sure of my lines - no one was there.

Don't you love farce? My fault, I fear
I thought that you'd want what I want -
Sorry, my dear
But where are the clowns?
Quick, send in the clowns
Don't bother they're here.

Isn't it rich, isn't it queer
Losing my timing this late in my career?
And where are the clowns?
There ought to be clowns
Well, maybe next year.

Unchained Melody
North/Zaret.

Oh, my love, my darling,
I've hungered for your touch
A long lonely time
Time goes by so slowly
And time can do so much,
Are you still mine?

I need your love, I need your love,
God speed your love to me!

Lonely rivers flow to the sea, to the sea,
To the open arms of the sea.
Lonely rivers sigh "Wait for me, wait for me".
I'll be coming home, wait for me!

It's Now Or Never
Schroeder/Gold

Refrain
It's now or never,
come hold me tight
Kiss me my darling,
be mine tonight
Tomorrow will be too late,
it's now or never
My love won't wait.

When I first saw you
with your smile so tender
My heart was captured,
my soul surrendered
I'd spend a life time
waiting for the right time
Now that you're near
the time is here at last.

Refrain

Just like a willow,
we would cry an ocean
If we lost true love
and sweet devotion
Your lips excite me,
let your arms invite me
For who knows when
we'll meet again this way.

Refrain

Somewhere My Love
from Dr. Zhivago

Somewhere my Love, there will be songs to sing,
Although the snow covers the hope of spring,
Somewhere a hill blossoms in green and gold,
And there are dreams, all that your heart can hold.

Some day we'll meet again my love
Some day whenever the spring breaks through.

You'll come to me out of the long ago,
Warm as the wind soft as the kiss of snow,
Till then my sweet think of me now and then,
God speed my love 'till you are mine again..

PARTY PIECES   SONGS

The Fields of Athenry
Words and Music by Pete St.John

By a lonely prison wall
I heard a young girl calling
Michael they are taking you away.
For you stole Travelyn's corn
So the young might see the morn,
Now a prison ship lies waiting in the bay.

Chorus
Low lie the fields of Athenry
Where once we watched the small free birds fly
Our love was on the wing,
We had dreams and songs to sing.
It's so lonely round the fields of Athenry.

By a lonely prison wall
I heard a young man calling
Nothing matters Mary when you're free,
Against the famine and the Crown
I rebelled they ran me down
Now you must raise our child with Dignity.

Chorus

By a lonely harbour wall
She watched the last star falling
As that prison ship sailed out against the sky
Sure she'll wait and hope and pray
For her love in Botany Bay
It's so lonely round the fields of Athenry.

Chorus

We'll meet again
Parker/Charles

We'll meet again don't know where
don't know when,
But I know we'll meet again some sunny day,
Keep smilin' thro' just like you always do
Till the blue skies drive the dark clouds far away.

So will you please say hello to the folks that I know,
Tell them I won't be long
They'll be happy to know that as you saw me go
I was singing this song

We'll meet again don't know where
don't know when,
But I know we'll meet again
some sunny day

43

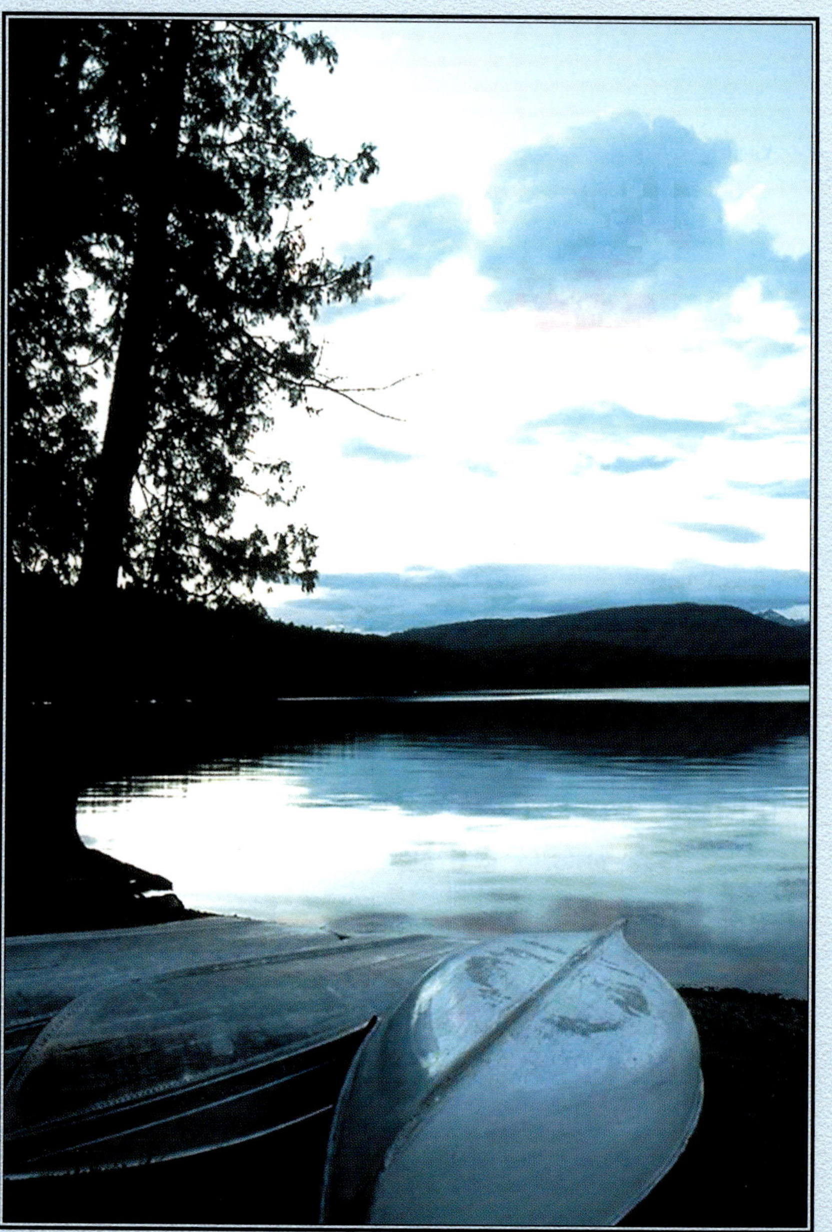

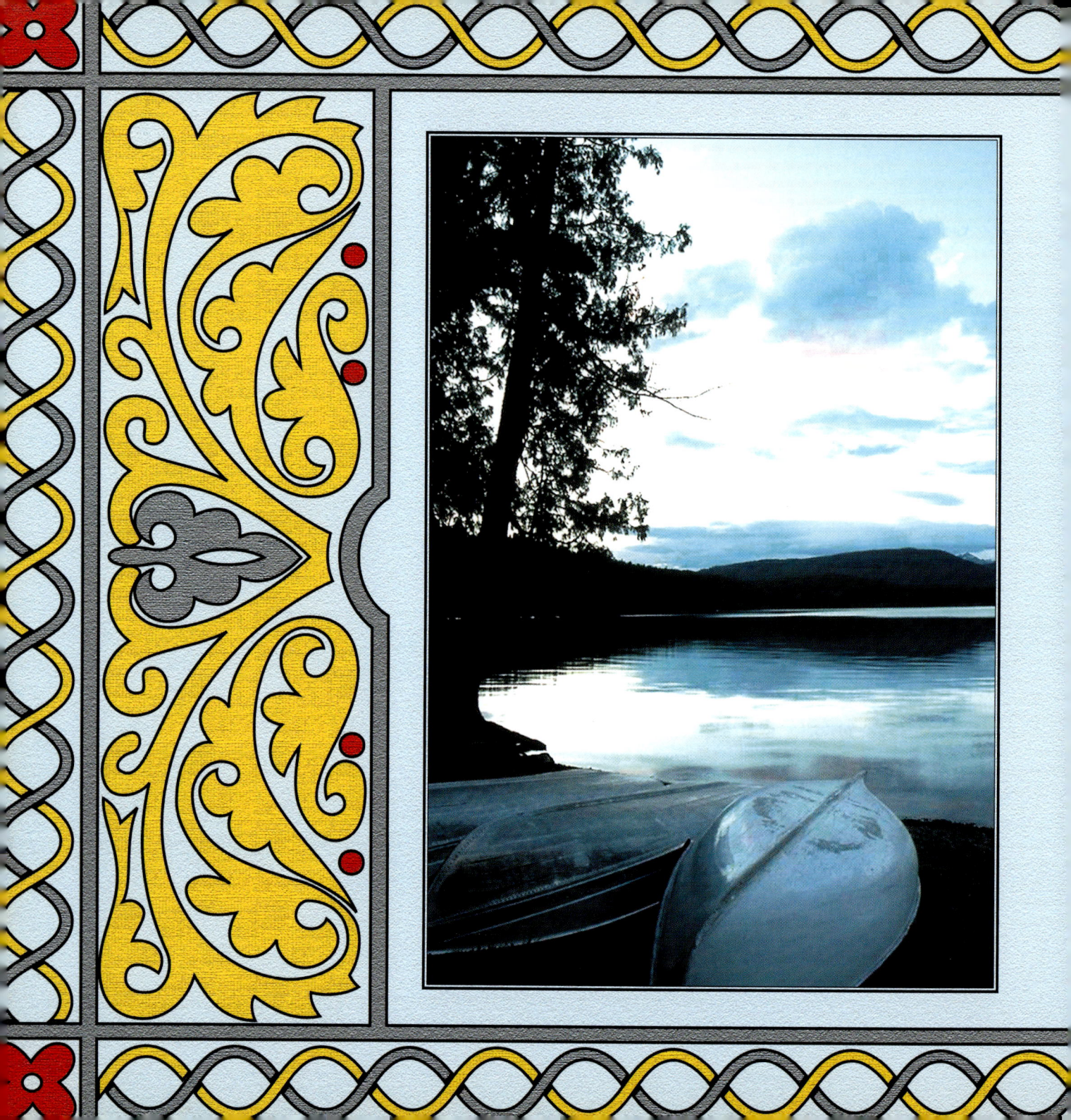

Poems

Poetry is "the food of love" and we all love to hear a good poem recited with real feeling. Here is a selection of long and short ones, some full of emotion, and others that are funny or serious.

Read through them all a few times and you will find some that appeal to you. These are the ones you choose. If you think of their meaning and feel the rhythm you will recite them well. Learn them off by heart - but if you think you might forget the words - bring this book and have it ready .... just in case!

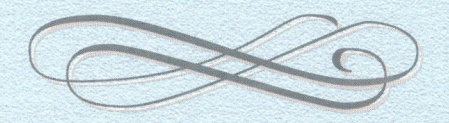

PARTY PIECES   POEMS

A Flea and a Fly

A flea and a fly in the flue
Were imprisoned so what could they do?
Said the fly, "Let us flee",
Said the flea, "Let us fly!"
So they flew through a flaw in the flue.

My Neighbour's Roses
A.L. Gruber

The roses red upon my neighbour's vine
Are owned by him, but they are also mine.
His was the cost, and his the labour, too.
Now I and he with joy,
Their loveliness can view.

They bloom for me and are for me as fair
As for the man who gives them all his care.
Thus I am rich because a good man grew
A rose-clad vine for all his neighbours' view.

I know from this, that others plant for me,
And what they own my joy may also be.
So why be selfish when so much that's fine
Is grown for you upon your neighbour's vine?

My Neighbour's Reply
Author Unknown

Your neighbour, sir, whose roses you admire
Is glad indeed to know that they inspire
Within your breast a feeling quite as fine
As felt by him who owns and tends that vine.

That those fair flowers should give my neighbours joy
But swells my own, and draws therefrom alloy
Which would lessen its full worth, did I not know
That others' pleasure in the flowers grow.

Friend, from my neighbours and this vine I've learned
That sharing pleasure means a profit turned
And he who shares the joy in what he's grown
Spreads joy abroad and doubles all his own

And here is

One Little Boy
Anon

I'm a little gentleman,
Play, and ride, and dance I can;
Very handsome clothes I wear,
And I live on dainty fare:
And whenever out I ride,
I've a servant by my side.

And I never, all the day,
Need do anything but play,
Nor even soil my little hand,
Because I am so very grand.
O! I'm very glad, I'm sure,
I need not labour, like the poor.

For I think I could not bear,
Such old shabby clothes to wear;
To lie upon so hard a bed,
And only live on barley bread;
And what is worse too, ev'ry day
To have to work as hard as they.

Another Little Boy
Anon

I'm a little husbandman,
Work and labour hard I can;
I'm as happy all the day
At my work as if 'twere play;
Tho' I've nothing fine to wear,
Yet for that I do not care.

When to work I go along,
Singing loud my morning song,
With my wallet at my back,
Or my waggon whip to smack;
O, I am as happy then,
As the idle gentleman.

I've a healthy appetite,
And I soundly sleep at night,
Down I lie content, and say,
"I've been useful all the day.
I'd rather be a plough-boy, than
A useless little gentleman."

Party Pieces — Poems

Evolution
Author Unknown

Three monkeys sat in a coconut tree
Discussing things as they're meant to be
Said one to the others, "Now listen, you two
There's a certain rumour that can't be true!
That man decended from our noble race
The very Idea! It's a disgrace.

Has Mr. Monkey ever deserted his wife,
Starved his baby, and ruined his life?
And you have never known a mother monk
To leave her baby with another to bunk.
Or pass him on from one to another,
Till he hardly knows who is his mother!

Another thing you never will see
A monk build a fence round a coconut tree!
And let the coconuts go to waste
Forbidding all other monks to taste.
Why, if I put a fence around this tree,
Starvation would force them to steal from me.

Here's another thing a monk won't do
Go out at night and get on a stew,
Or use a weapon, gun, or knife
To take from him some other monk's life.
Yes, man descended, the onery cuss!
But Brother, he didn't descend from us!"

He Wishes for the Cloths of Heaven
W.B. Yeats

Had I the heavens' embroidered cloths,
Enwrought with golden and silver light,
The blue and the dim and the dark cloths
Of night and light and the half-light,
I would spread the cloths under your feet:
But I, being poor, have only my dreams;
I have spread my dreams under your feet;
Tread softly because you tread on my dreams.

The People Upstairs
Ogden Nash

The people upstairs all practise ballet.
Their living room is a bowling alley.
Their bedroom is full of conducted tours.
Their radio is louder than yours.
They celebrate weekends all the week.
When they take a shower, your ceilings leak.
They try to get their parties to mix
By supplying their guests with Pogo sticks.
And when their orgy at last abates,
They go to the bathroom on roller skates.
I might love the people upstairs wondrous
If instead of above us, they just lived under us.

Golf is ....

Anne C. Duffy, The Rhyming Rabbit

Golf is ......
A game, a sport, a way of life;
It's exercise, it's a break from the wife!
Golf is .....
Frustrating,
At times nauseating
When those short putts don't go in.
But it's
Pulsating
Invigorating
When, just for once, we win.

We love it, we hate it
We heartily relate it.
Our non-golfing friends we bore.
We love it, we hate it
But we can't escape it;
We get caught in it's grip once more.

Golf is .....
An affliction
A painful addiction;
Should be listed a dangerous drug.
We get so high,
Like the golf balls we sky
When we're bitten by the bug.

We hate it; we adore it
But we can't ignore it;
Once a golf club we have swung
We hate it; we adore it;
We eagerly folk-lore it,
We lose, but the game has won.

Golf is ......
A touch of magic;
A hint of the tragic,
It's everything life's made of.
Though words don't describe it
Let no fool deride it.
It's the game we love....
It's Golf!

I'm The Dog Who Didn't Win A Prize
Pam Ayres

I'm the dog who didn't win a prize
I didn't have the Most Appealing Eyes,
All day in this heat, I've been standing on my feet
With dogs of every other shape and size.

I've been harshly disinfected, I've been scrubbed
I've been festooned in a towel and I've been rubbed
I've been mercilessly brushed, robbed of all my fleas and dust
And now the judging's over: I've been snubbed.

Was it for obedience I was hailed?
As 'Best Dog in the Show' was I regaled?
O not on your Doggo Life, pass me down the carving knife,
I had one thing said about me - it was *'failed'*

I never for a moment thought I'd fail
I thought at least I'd win 'Waggiest Tail'
But no certificate, rosette or commendation did I get -
Nothing on the kennel door to nail.

I am going in my kennel on my own
Thank you no, I do not want a bone.
Do not think you can console me with left-overs in my bowl
My pride is mortified - I want to be alone.

I've heard it from the worldly and the wise:
'Each dog has his day' they all advise,
But I see to my grief and sorrow,
My day must have been tomorrow!
Oh I'm the dog who didn't win a prize!

My Time of Day
James J. Metcalfe

The time of day I like the best
Is that of early dawn
When night has disappeared and when
The shadows all are gone.

The sun may rise, or it may be
A cloudy, rainy day.
It matters not too much to me,
I like it either way.

I mean, I like the quietude
On street and avenue.
The morning air so clean and fresh
And life so bright and new.

It is the time to turn my thoughts
To heaven and to earth
And to evaluate my soul
For what it may be worth.

According to accomplishments
Or failures of the past
And thank my God because He has
Allowed my life to last.

Hugs
Author Unknown

It's wondrous what a hug can do.
A hug can cheer you when you're blue.
A hug can say "I love you so"
Or, "I hate to see you go".
A hug is "Welcome back again" and
"Great to see you! Where've you been?"
A hug can soothe a small child's pain,
And bring a rainbow after rain.
The hug, there's just no doubt about it -
We scarcely could survive without it!
A hug delights and warms and charms,
It must be why God gave us arms.

Hugs are great for fathers and mothers
Sweet for sisters, swell for brothers.
And chances are your favourite aunts
Love them more than potted plants.
Kittens crave them, puppies love them,
Heads of state are not above them.
A hug can break the language barrier,
And make travel so much merrier.
No need to fret about your store of 'em
The more you give, there's more of 'em.
So stretch those arms without delay.
And give someone a hug today!

Visit the Sick
James J. Metcalfe

There is no person lonelier than he who lies in bed
And must depend on others to be comfortable and fed,
Who never has a visitor to talk to him and smile,
And make the life he has to live, a little more worth while.

He does not ask for magazines, nor candy, fruit and such,
But just a friendly visit and the words that mean so much.
He wants to see the sun come out in place of all the rain,
And know that someone cares about his trouble and his pain.

And surely somewhere out of all the moments made for play,
There must be time to call on him and say 'hello' today.

Adipose Auntie's Pose
Anon

Auntie always was morose
And her views on life were bitter,
For she was so adipose
No ordinary seat would fit'er:
Now I should think that you'd feel glum
If you'd been born with Auntie's "sitter"

A Piper
Seumas O'Sullivan

A Piper in the street today,
Set up, and tuned, and started to play,
And away, away, away on the tide
Of his music we started; on every side
Doors and windows were opened wide,
And men left down their work and came,
And women with petticoats coloured like flame,
And little bare feet that were blue with cold,
Went dancing back to the age of gold,
And all the world went gay, went gay,
For half an hour in the street to-day.

Leisure
W.H. Davies

What is this life if, full of care,
We have no time to stand and stare.

No time to stand beneath the boughs
And stare as long as sheep or cows.

No time to see, when woods we pass,
Where squirrels hide their nuts in grass

No time to see, in broad daylight,
Streams full of stars, like skies at night.

No time to turn at Beauty's glance,
And watch her feet, how they can dance.

No time to wait till her mouth can
Enrich that smile her eyes began.

A poor life this if, full of care,
We have no time to stand and stare.

The Daffodils
W. Wordsworth

I wander'd lonely as a cloud
That floats on high o'er vales and hills,
When all at once I saw a crowd,
A host of golden daffodils,
Beside the lake, beneath the trees
Fluttering and dancing in the breeze.

Continuous as the stars that shine
And twinkle on the milky way,
They stretched in never-ending line
Along the margin of a bay:
Ten thousand saw I at a glance
Tossing their heads in sprightly dance.

The waves beside them danced, but they
Out-did the sparkling waves in glee:-
A Poet could not but be gay
In such a jocund company!
I gazed - and gazed - but little thought
What wealth the show to me had brought;

For oft, when on my couch I lie
In vacant or in pensive mood,
They flash upon that inward eye
Which is the bliss of solitude;
And then my heart with pleasure fills,
And dances with the daffodils.

PARTY PIECES   POEMS

PARTY PIECES   POEMS

George The Giraffe
Jeremy Lloyd

Young George the Giraffe
Used to wear a big scarf
And in winter time donned a warm coat.
For he lived in a zoo
And had twice caught the flu,
And often he had a sore throat.
So far from his home
He'd stand there alone
And dream of the African plain,
Where he'd lived as a lad
With his mum and his dad
And he wished he could see them again.
For life in a zoo
When you're prone to the flu
And you've got the world's longest sore throat,
Despite thick pyjamas
And lots of bananas,
Makes you want to get on the next boat.
So next time you go to the zoo
And they show
Every animal there except one,
A lonely giraffe, in a coat and a scarf,
It means George has escaped to the sun.

Your Neighbour
H. Howard Biggar

Do you know the neighbour who lives in your block;
Do you ever take time for a bit of a talk?
Do you know his troubles, his heartaches, his cares,
The battles he's fighting, the burdens he bears?

Do you greet him with joy or pass him right by
With a questioning look and a quizzical eye?
Do you bid him "Good Morning" and "How do you do,"
Or shrug up as if he was nothing to you?

He may be a chap with a mighty big heart,
And a welcome that grips, if you just do your part.
And I know you'll coax out his sunniest smile,
If you'll stop with this neighbour and visit awhile.

The Lake Isle of Innisfree
W.B. Yeats

I will arise and go now, and go to Innisfree,
And a small cabin build there, of clay and wattles made:
Nine bean-rows will I have there, a hive for the honey-bee,
And live alone in the bee-loud glade.

And I shall have some peace there, for peace comes dropping slow,
Dropping from the veils of the morning to where the cricket sings;
There midnight's all a glimmer, and noon a purple glow,
And evening full of the linnet's wings.

I will arise and go now for always night and day
I hear lake water lapping with low sounds by the shore;
While I stand on the roadway, on the pavements grey,
I hear it in the deep heart's core.

Down by the Salley Gardens
W.B. Yeats.

Down by the salley gardens my love and I did meet;
She passed the salley gardens with little snow-white feet.
She bid me take love easy, as the leaves grow on the tree;
But I, being young and foolish, with her would not agree.

In a field by the river my love and I did stand,
And on my leaning shoulder she laid her snow-white hand.
She bid me take life easy, as the grass grows on the weirs;
But I was young and foolish, and now am full of tears.

An Old Woman of the Roads
Padraic Colum

Oh, to have a little house!
To own the hearth and stool and all!
The heaped-up sods upon the fire,
The pile of turf against the wall!

To have a clock with weights and chains
And pendulum swinging up and down!
A dresser filled with shining delph,
Speckled and white and blue and brown!

I could be busy all the day
Clearing and sweeping hearth and floor
And fixing on their shelf again
My white and blue and speckled store!

I could be quiet there at night
Beside the fire and by myself,
Sure of a bed, and loth to leave
The ticking clock and the shining delph!

Och! but I'm weary of mist and dark,
And roads where there's never a house or bush,
And tired I am of bog and road
And the crying wind and the lonesome hush!

And I am praying to God on high,
And I am praying Him night and day,
For a little house - a house of my own -
Out of the wind's and the rain's way.

The Way We Tell a Story
Pat McCarty

Says I to him, I says, says I,
Says I to him, I says,
The thing, says I, I says to him,
Is just, says I, this ways.
I hev', says I, a gret respeck
For you and for your breed,
And onything I cud, I says,
I'd do, I wud indeed.
I don't know any man, I says,
I'd do it for, says I,
As fast, I says, as for yoursel',
That's tellin' ye no lie.
There's nought, says I, I wudn't do
To plase your feyther's son,
But this, I says, ye see, says I,
I says, it can't be done.

"If I was a Lady".
Percy French

If I was a lady, I'd wear a hat,
That all the street would be lookin' at.
An' I'd have a ladies' maid, d'ye mind,
To lace and button me dress behind.
A dress that was lined with good sateen,
None o' yer bits o' bombazine,
And the girls with envy would grind their teeth,
When they heard it rustling underneath.
If I was a lady - but then I'm not,
This shawl is the dacentest thing I've got.

If I was lady I'd drive to the play,
An' I'd look through me opera glass and say -
"I've seen this silly revue before,
The leading lady's an awful bore;
Let's all get up when she starts her song,
An' go an' eat cakes in a resterong."
Then a powder puff on me nose I'd dab,
An' drive off home in a taxi cab,
If I was a lady - but then I'm not,
A pass to the gallery's all I've got.

If I was a lady - a regular swell,
With a hairy boa, an' a silk umbrel',
'Tis me that would walk into Shelbourne's Hotel,
An' order me dinner - "Some pork an' beans,
An' whatever ye've got in them soup turreens,
Both the sweets, an' a hunk o' cheese,
And oh, a bottle o 'porter please."
Then I'd call for me bill and setteling it,
I'd give the waiter a threepenny bit,
If I was a lady - but then I'm not,
- My dinner comes out o' the stirabout pot.
Still there's a lot of show and sham,
Maybe I'm safer the way I am.

The Horse's Farewell to His Cowboy
Pam Ayres

Farewell to you cowboy, my day it is done,
Of rounding up cows in the heat of the sun
Of roping the dogies and branding the steer
And having your gun going off in my ear.
I galloped the prairie without any thanks
Your great silver spurs in my bony old flanks
And I've seen many things in my life it is true
But never a cowboy more stupid than you.

Cowboy can you hear me inside the saloon?
I'm waiting out here in the light of the moon,
My hardworking days they are past and gone by,
And I'm bound for the great clover field in the sky.

Farewell to the feel of your filthy old jeans
Farewell to the smell of your coffee and beans
Farewell to you in your stetson and chaps,
Cheating at poker and shooting the craps.
You rode me too fast and you rode me too far,
Mile after mile of you shouting "Yee Har!"
Hounded by outlaws away down the track,
With a gun on my tail and a berk on my back.

I never remember you treating me right,
I was tied to a cactus and hungry all night,
When I was weary and dying of thirst,
I always knew it was you who came first.
Well maybe you are mighty quick on the draw,
But cowboy you're slow with the fodder and straw.
Look at me pardner, I'm all skin and bone,
So tonight I ride into the sunset ...... alone.

He'll have a shock when he comes out of there,
Me, with four legs sticking up in the air,
Don't say goodbye or thanks for the ride,
My friend it's too little too late. I have died.
Won't somebody lift up the old saddle flaps,
My eyes have grown weary, I'm tired of talk,
And as from tonight, he can bloody well walk.

PARTY PIECES   POEMS

Mary - the lamb and the bear

Mary had a little lamb,
She ate it with mint sauce,
And everywhere that Mary went
The lamb went too, of course.

Mary had a little bear
To which she was so kind
That everywhere dear Mary went
You saw her bear ...... running along beside her!

Erasers
Author unknown

Erasers are the nicest things!
Of that there is no doubt.
We write wrong words, a few quick swipes-
And big mistakes fade out ...
And you will find erasers,
Of a very different kind,
Extremely helpful, if you try
To bear these facts in mind:
When you bump into somebody
And almost knock her down,
A soft "I'm sorry!" may bring smiles
And rub out that old frown.
Apologies, invariably,
Obliterate mistakes;
And three small words, "I love you!"
Can erase the worst heartaches.

The Poem
Nuala Harnett

You asked me to say a short poem,
But right now I feel all alone;
My scalp starts to tighten
The more I get frightened
Why didn't I just stay at home.

Oh, I wish I'd looked after me Teeth
Pam Ayres

Oh, I wish I'd looked after me teeth,
And spotted the perils beneath
All the toffees I chewed,
And the sweet sticky food.
Oh, I wish I'd looked after me teeth.

I wish I'd been that much more willin'
When I had more tooth there than fillin'
To give up gobstoppers,
From respect to me choppers,
And to buy something else with me shillin'.

When I think of the lollies I licked
And the liquorice allsorts I picked,
Sherbet dabs, big and little,
All that hard peanut brittle,
My conscience gets horribly pricked.

My mother, she told me no end,
'If you got a tooth, you got a friend.'
I was young then, and careless,
My toothbrush was hairless,
I never had much time to spend.

Oh I showed them the toothpaste all right,
I flashed it about late at night,
But up-and-down brushin'
And pokin' and fussin'
Didn't seem worth the time - I could bite!

If I'd known I was paving the way
To cavities, caps and decay,
The murder of fillin's,
Injections and drillin's,
I'd have thrown all me sherbet away.

So I lay in the old dentist's chair
And I gaze up his nose in despair.
And his drill it do whine
In these molars of mine.
'Two amalgam', he'll say, 'for in there.'

How I laughed at my mother's false teeth,
As they foamed in the waters beneath.
But now comes the reckonin'
It's *me* they are beckonin'
Oh, I *wish* I'd looked after me teeth

Party Pieces   Poems

Ach, I Dunno!
Percy French

I'm simply surrounded by lovers
Since Da made his fortune in land.
They're comin' in crowds like the plovers
To ax for me hand -
There's clerks and policemen and teachers,
Some sandy, some black as a crow -
Ma says you get used to the creatures
But, ach, I dunno!

The convent is in a commotion
To think of me taking a spouse,
And they wonder I hadn't the notion
Of taking the vows.
'Tis a beautiful life and a quiet,
And keeps ye from going below,
As a girl I thought I might try it,
But, ach, I dunno!

I've none but meself to look after,
An' marriage it fills me with fears,
I think I'd have less of the laughter
And more of the tears.
I'll not be a slave like me mother,
With six of us all in a row,
Even one little baby's a bother,
But, ach, I dunno!

There's a lad that has taken me fancy,
I know he's a bit of a limb,
And though marriage is terrible chancy,
I'd - chance it with him.
He's coming tonight - oh - I tingle,
From the top of me head to me toe,
I'll tell him I'd rather live single,
But, ach, I dunno!

Lil of Kilquade

Cosmetically Lil of Kilquade
Had beauty that ne'er seemed to fade.
When tanned by the sun
She looked twenty-one,
But she looked fifty-six in the shade.

If
R. Kipling

If you can keep your head when all about you
Are losing theirs and blaming it on you;
If you can trust yourself when all men doubt you,
But make allowance for their doubting too;
If you can wait and not be tired by waiting,
Or being lied about, don't deal in lies,
Or being hated don't give way to hating,
And yet don't look too good, nor talk too wise;

If you can dream - and not make dreams your master;
If you can think - and not make thoughts your aim,
If you can meet with Triumph and Disaster
And treat those two impostors just the same;
If you can bear to hear the truth you've spoken
Twisted by knaves to make a trap for fools,
Or watch the things you gave your life to, broken,
And stoop and build 'em up with work-out tools;

If you can make one heap of all your winnings
And risk it on one turn of pitch-and-toss,
And lose, and start again at your beginnings
And never breathe a word about your loss;
If you can force your heart and nerve and sinew
To serve your turn long after they are gone,
And so hold on when there is nothing in you
Except the Will which says to them:- 'Hold on!'

If you can talk with crowds and keep your virtue,
Or walk with Kings - nor lose the common touch,
If neither foes nor loving friends can hurt you,
If all men count with you, but none too much;
If you can fill the unforgiving minute
With sixty seconds' worth of distance run,
Yours is the Earth and everything that's in it,
And - which is more - you'll be a Man, my son!

A Pint of Plain is your Only Man
Flann O'Brien

When things go wrong and will not come right,
Though you do the best you can,
When life looks black as the hour of night -
A pint of plain is your only man.

When money's tight and is hard to get
And your horse has also ran,
When all you have is a heap of debt -
A pint of plain is your only man.

When health is bad and your heart feels strange,
And your face is pale and wan,
When doctors say that you need a change -
A pint of plain is your only man.

When food is scarce and your larder bare
And no rashers grease your pan,
When hunger grows as your meals are rare -
A pint of plain is your only man.

In time of trouble and lousy strife,
You have still got a darlint plan,
You still can turn to a brighter life -
A pint of plain is your only man.

Tell Him Now
Source Unknown

If with pleasure you are viewing
Any work a man is doing,
If you like him if you love him
Tell him now.
Do not withhold your admiration
Till the clergy make oration
And he lies with snowy lilies o'er his brow.
For then no matter how you shout it
He won't really care about it,
He won't know how many teardrops you have shed.
So if you think some praise is due him
Now is the time to give it to him.
He cannot read his tombstone when he's dead.

A Noble Boy
Author Unknown

The woman was old, and feeble, and grey,
And bent with the chill of the winter's day;
The street was wet with the recent snow,
And the woman's feet were weary and slow.
She stood at the crossing, and waited long,
Alone, uncared for, amid the throng.
Down the street, with laughter and shout,
Glad in the freedom of 'school let out',
Came the boys, like a flock of sheep;
Hailing the snow, piled white and deep.
Past the woman, so old and grey,
Hastened the children on their way,
Nor offered a helping hand to her,
So meek, so timid, afraid to stir.

At last came one of the merry troop -
The gayest boy of all the group;
He paused beside her, and whispered low,
'I'll help you across if you wish to go'.
He guided the trembling feet along,
Proud, that his own were firm and strong.
Then back again to his friends, he went,
His young heart happy, and well content,
'She is somebody's mother, boys, you know,
Although she is old, and poor and slow,
And I hope some fellow will lend a hand
To help my mother - you understand -
If e'er she be poor, and old and grey,
When her own dear boy is far away'.

And 'somebody's mother' bowed low her head,
In her home that night, and the prayer she said
Was 'God be kind to the noble boy,
Who is somebody's son, and pride, and joy'.

The Pig
Anon

It was an evening in November,
As I very well remember,
I was strolling down the street in drunken pride,
But my knees were all a-flutter,
And I landed in the gutter
And a pig came up and lay down by my side.

Yes, I lay there in the gutter
Thinking thoughts I could not utter,
When a colleen passing by did softly say
'You can tell a man who boozes
By the company he chooses' -
And the pig got up and slowly walked away.

Indispensable
Anonymous

Sometime, when you're feeling important,
Sometime, when your ego's in bloom,
Sometime, when you take it for granted,
You're the best qualified man in the room;
Sometime when you feel that your going
Would leave an unfillable hole,
Just follow this simple instruction,
And see how it humbles your soul.

Take a bucket and fill it with water,
Put your hand in it up to the wrist;
Pull it out; and the hole that's remaining,
Is a measure of how you'll be missed.
You may splash all you please, when you enter,
You can stir up the water galore,
But stop, and you'll find in a minute,
That it looks quite the same as before.

The moral in this quaint example,
Is do just the best you can,
Be proud of yourself but remember,
There's no indispensable man.

Around the Corner
Charles Hanson Towne

Around the corner I have a friend,
In this great city that has no end;
Yet days go by, and weeks rush on,
And before I know it a year is gone.

And I never see my old friend's face,
For life is a swift and terrible race.
He knows I like him just as well
As in the days when I rang his bell.

And he rang mine. We were younger then,
And now we are busy, tired men:
Tired with playing a foolish game,
Tired with trying to make a name.

"Tomorrow." I say, "I will call on Jim,
Just to show that I'm thinking of him."
But tomorrow comes - and tomorrow goes,
And the distance between us grows and grows.

Around the corner! - yet miles away.....
"Here's a telegram, sir...."
"Jim died today."
And that's what we get, and deserve in the end:
Around the corner, a vanished friend.

On a Tired Housewife
Anon

Here lies a poor woman who was always tired,
She lived in a house where help wasn't hired;
Her last words on earth were: "Dear friends I am going
To where there's no cooking, or washing, or sewing,
For everything there is exact to my wishes,
For where they don't eat there's no washing of dishes.
I'll be where loud anthems will always be ringing,
But having no voice I'll be quit of the singing.
Don't mourn for me now, don't mourn for me never,
I am going to do nothing for ever and ever".

Work
J.W. Thompson.

How true it is when I am sad,
A little work can make me glad.
When frowning care comes to my door,
I work a while and fret no more.
I leave my couch harassed with pain,
I work, and soon I'm well again.
When sorrow comes and vain regret,
I go to work and soon forget.
Work soothes the soul when joys depart,
And often mends a broken heart.
The idle mind soon fills with murk,
So that's why God invented work.

Christmas Greetings
Author Unknown

I have a list of folks I know, all written in a book
And every year at Christmas time I go and take a look
And that is when I realize that these names are all a part
Not of the book they're written in but of my very heart.

For each name stands for someone who has crossed my path sometime.
And in that meeting they've become the "Rhythm of the Rhyme"
And while it sounds fantastic for me to make this claim
I really feel I am composed of Each Remembered Name.

And while you may not be aware of any special link
Just meeting you shaped my life more than you can think
For once you've met somebody, the years cannot erase
The memory of a pleasant word or of a friendly face.

So Never think My Christmas Cards are just a mere routine,
Of names upon a Christmas list forgotten in between.
For when I send a Christmas card that is addressed to you
It's because you're on that list of folks I am indebted to.

For we are but a total of the many folks we've met
And you happen to be one of those I prefer not to forget.
And whether I have known you for many years or few
In some way you have had a part in shaping things I do.

And every year when Christmas comes I realize anew
The biggest gift that life can give is meeting folks like you.
And may the spirit of Christmas that forever and ever endures
Leave its richest blessings in the heart of you and yours.

PARTY PIECES POEMS

Poor Beasts
Anon

The horse and mule live 30 years
And nothing know of wine and beers.
The goat and sheep at 20 die
And never taste of Scotch or Rye.

The cow drinks water by the ton
And at 18 is mostly done.
The dog at 15 cashes in
Without the aid of rum and gin.

The cat in milk and water soaks
And then in 12 short years it croaks.
The modest, sober, bone-dry hen
Lays eggs for nogs, then dies at 10.

All animals are strictly dry,
They sinless live and swiftly die.
But sinful, ginful, rum-soaked men
Survive for three score years and ten,
And some of them, a very few,
Stay pickled till they're 92.

Lay not up
L.W.G.

The bees
Sneeze and wheeze
    Scraping pollen and honey
From the lime trees:

The ants
Hurries and pants
    Storing up everything
They wants:

But the flies
Is wise
    When the cold weather comes
They dies.

First Parting
Alice Taylor

It hurts me so
To see him thus
My babe
Of tender years,
Clutching
At his little sack,
Choking back
His tears.
I long to shelter
In my arms
This little lad
Turned four,
But I will
Take him by the hand
And lead
Him out the door.
Into a world
Where he must have
The courage
To stand alone,
Strengthened
By the love
That he has known
At home.
And I must learn
To let him go
Though helping
When I can,
My little son
Now taking
His first steps
To being
A man.

Please Call
Alice Taylor

I am old,
I live alone:
Please don't leave me
On my own.
I sit on a chair,
I lie in bed,
Voluntary services keep me fed.
This is where I would be:
Please, please, call on me.
The clock goes tick,
The clock goes tock,
Please turn the key
That's in the lock.
The time is long,
The time goes slow;
Long hours alone,
I'm feeling low.
Please come
And chat awhile,
The human touch
Will make me smile.

Together
Author Unknown

You were born together and together you shall be for evermore. You shall be together when the white wings of death scatter your days. Yes, you shall be together even in the silent memory of God. But let there be spaces in your togetherness. And let the winds of the heavens dance between you. Love one another, but make not a bond of love: Let it rather be a moving sea between the shores of your souls. Sing and dance together and be joyous, but let each one of you be alone. Even as the strings of a lute are alone though they quiver with the same music. Stand together, yet not too near together, for the pillars of the temple stand apart. And the oak tree and cypress grow not in each other's shadow.

Chains
Alice Taylor

I saw a bird
Upon a tree,
I smiled at him
 He sang to me
And said "Will you come today,
Come with me and fly away
Across the silent ocean wide,
Over yawning mountainside?
You will see the things that be,
That thrill my heart
And make me free."
I said, "I have things to do
So I cannot fly with you,"
He looked at me
In a sad way
And sang "You cannot fly today,
Because you're busy doing things,
You will never fly on wings.
You cannot soar above the sound,
You belong on solid ground".

Middle Age
Author Unknown

Maybe it's true that life begins at fifty. But everything else starts to wear out, fall out, or spread out.

There are three signs of old age. The first is your loss of memory. The other two I forget.

Middle age is when it takes longer to rest than to get tired.

By the time a man is wise enough to watch his step, he's too old to go anywhere.

Middle age is having a choice of two temptations - and choosing the one that will get you home earlier.

You know you're into middle age when you realize that caution is the only thing you care to exercise.

Don't worry about avoiding temptation. As you grow older, it will avoid you.

You're getting old when getting lucky means you find your car in the parking lot.

You're getting old when you're sitting in a rocker and you can't get it started.

You're getting old when your wife gives up sex for Lent, and you don't know till the 4th July.

It's hard to be nostalgic when you can't remember anything.

You know your getting old when you stop buying green bananas.

Jim
Alice Taylor

Just across the road
Jim lived in a shed;
It wasn't very big,
Just enough to hold his bed.
He was never lonely,
He chatted on the street,
A kindly neighbour fed him
So he had enough to eat.
But it didn't seem right
Him sleeping in the cold;
Something should be done
As Jim was getting old.
So he went into a home
Where everything was right,
And everyone felt good
Now Jim was in by night.
But when I went to see him
His face a story told;
His body was dry and warm
But his eyes were lost and cold.
Jim had lived here too long
To dig up his ancient roots;
His body now had comfort
But his heart was in his boots.
Jim died then in September,
Died in a spotless bed,
But he had died six months before,
The day he left the shed.

Desiderata
Found in old Saint Paul's Church, Baltimore: Dated 1692

Go placidly amid the noise and haste,
and remember what peace there may be in silence.
As far as possible without surrender
be on good terms with all persons.
Speak your truth quietly and clearly;
and listen to others, even the dull and ignorant;
they too have their story.
Avoid loud and aggressive persons,
they are vexations to the spirit.
If you compare yourself with others,
you may become vain and bitter; for always
there will be greater and lesser persons than yourself.
Enjoy your achievements as well as your plans.
Keep interested in your own career, however humble;
it is a real possession in the changing fortunes of time.
Exercise caution in your business affairs;
for the world is full of trickery.
But let this not blind you to what virtue there is;
many persons strive for high ideals;
and everywhere life is full of heroism.
Be yourself. Especially, do not feign affection.
Neither be cynical about love;
for in the face of all aridity and disenchantment
it is perennial as the grass.
Take kindly the counsel of the years,
gracefully surrendering the things of youth.
Nurture strength of spirit to shield you in sudden misfortune.
But do not distress yourself with imaginings.
Many fears are born of fatigue and loneliness.
Beyond a wholesome discipline, be gentle with yourself.
You are a child of the universe,
no less than the trees and the stars;
you have a right to be here.
And whether or not it is clear to you,
no doubt the universe is unfolding as it should.
Therefore be at peace with God,
whatever you conceive Him to be,
and whatever your labors and aspirations,
in the noisy confusion of life keep peace with your soul.
With all its sham, drudgery and broken dreams,
it is still a beautiful world.
Be careful. Strive to be happy.

If I Had My Life To Live Over
Nadine Stair

If I had my life to live over I'd dare to make
more mistakes next time. I'd relax, I would limber up.
I would be sillier than I have been on this trip.
I would take fewer things seriously, I would take
more chances. I would climb more mountains and swim more rivers.
I would eat more ice cream and less beans. I would
perhaps have more actual troubles, but I'd have
fewer imaginary ones.

You see, I'm one of those people who lives sensibly
and sanely hour after hour, day after day. Oh, I've
had my moments, and if I had it to do over again
I'd have more of them. In fact, I'd try to have
nothing else. Just moments, one after another,
instead of living so many years ahead of each day.
I've been one of those persons who never goes
anywhere without a thermometer, a hot water bottle,
a rain coat, and a parachute. If I had to do it again,
I would travel lighter than I have.

If I had my life to live over, I would start barefoot
earlier in the spring and stay that way later in the
fall. I would go to more dances. I would ride more
merry-go-rounds. I would pick more daisies.

An Irish Toast

May there always be work for your hands to do
May your purse always hold a coin or two
May the sun always shine on your windowpane
May the rainbow be certain to follow each rain
May the hand of a friend always be near you
May God fill your heart with gladness, and cheer you.

An Irish Toast

May the road rise up to meet you
And may the wind always be at your back
May the sun shine warm upon your face
And the raindrops fall soft upon your fields
And until we meet again
May God hold you in the small of His hand.

Looking the Part
Anne C. Duffy - The Rhyming Rabbit.

I'm heading for the golf course,
I know I'm looking smart.
My bank account has come off worst,
But I really LOOK THE PART.

In my bag, my clubs look good
All matched in white and blue.
My shoes are right to the last stud
And yes, they're matching too.

I pull my clubs to the tee
In my shining new golf cart
And everything about me
Really LOOKS THE PART.

I have on the latest gear,
Everything is in THE style
But before you let out a cheer,
Pause and wait a while.....

I'm standing there on the tee,
And I'm about to start..
But.....
   My swing
      is the only thing about me
         That doesn't LOOK THE PART.

My Son the Bridegroom
Nuala Harnett

You are a fine and wonderful person
I'm lucky to have such a son,
Just stay as you are and be true to yourself
You have it all, and a gem of a wife.

Look to the stars and shine bright as the sun
Write a book or make music, but have fun.
It's your life, do just as you will
As long as yourself you fulfill.

Your family is right behind you
* Dad, Susan, Philip and I
Fly away now and build your own nest
* With Michelle, we know you've the best.

* change names as appropriate

Castaway
Anon

He grabbed me round my slender neck,
I could not shout or scream,
He carried me into his room
Where we could not be seen.
He tore away my flimsy wrap
And gazed upon my form -
I was so cold and still and damp,
While he was wet and warm.
His feverish mouth he pressed to mine -
I let him have his way -
He drained me of my very self,
I could not say him nay.
He made me what I am. Alas!
That's why you find me here......
A broken vessel - broken glass -
That once held Bottled Beer

Spring in the Bronx
Anon

Spring is sprung
Duh grass is riz
I wonder where dem boidies is.

Duh little boids is on duh wing -
But dat's absoid:
Duh little wing is on duh boid.

The English Language
Harry Hemsley

Some words have different meanings
   and yet they're spelled the same
A cricket is an insect,
   to play it - it's a game.
On every hand, in every land,
   It's thoroughly agreed,
The English language to explain,
   is very hard indeed.

Some people say that your'e a dear,
   yet dear is far from cheap.
A jumper is a thing you wear,
   yet a jumper has to leap.
It's very clear, it's very queer,
   and, pray, who is to blame
For different meanings to some words
   pronounced and spelled the same?

A little journey is a trip,
   a trip is when you fall.
It doesn't mean you have to dance
   whene'er you hold a ball.
Now here's a thing that puzzles me:
   musicians of good taste
Will very often form a band -
   I've one around my waist!

You spin a top, go for a spin,
   or spin a yarn maybe -
Yet every spin's a different spin
   as you can plainly see.
Now here's a most peculiar thing,
   'twas told me as a joke -
A dumb man wouldn't speak a word,
   yet seized a wheel and spoke!

A door may often be ajar,
   but give the door a slam
And then your nerves receive a jar -
   and then there's jars of jam.
You've heard, of course, of traffic jams,
   and jams you give your thumbs.
And adders, too, one is a snake,
   the other adds up sums.

A policeman is a copper,
   It's a nickname (impolite!)
Yet a copper in the kitchen
   is an article you light.
On every hand, in every land,
   it's thoroughly agreed,
The English language to explain
   is very hard indeed!

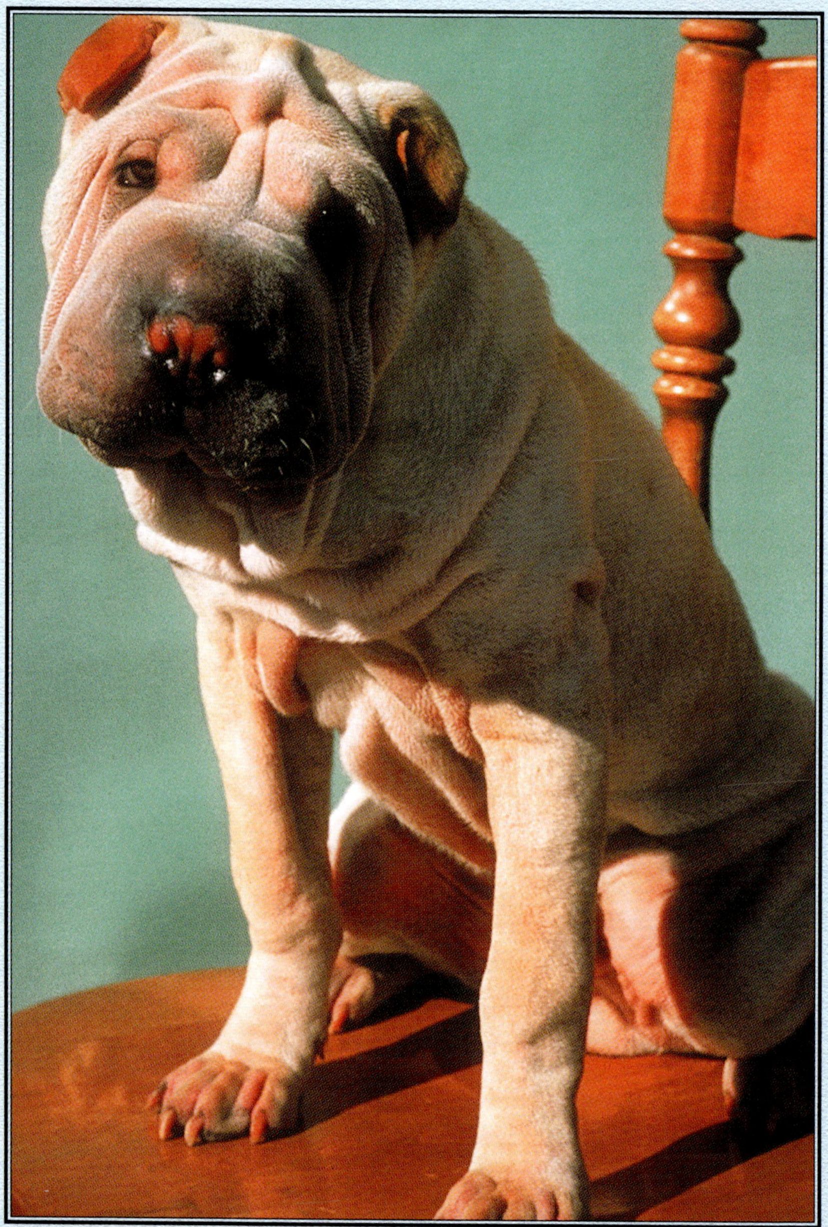

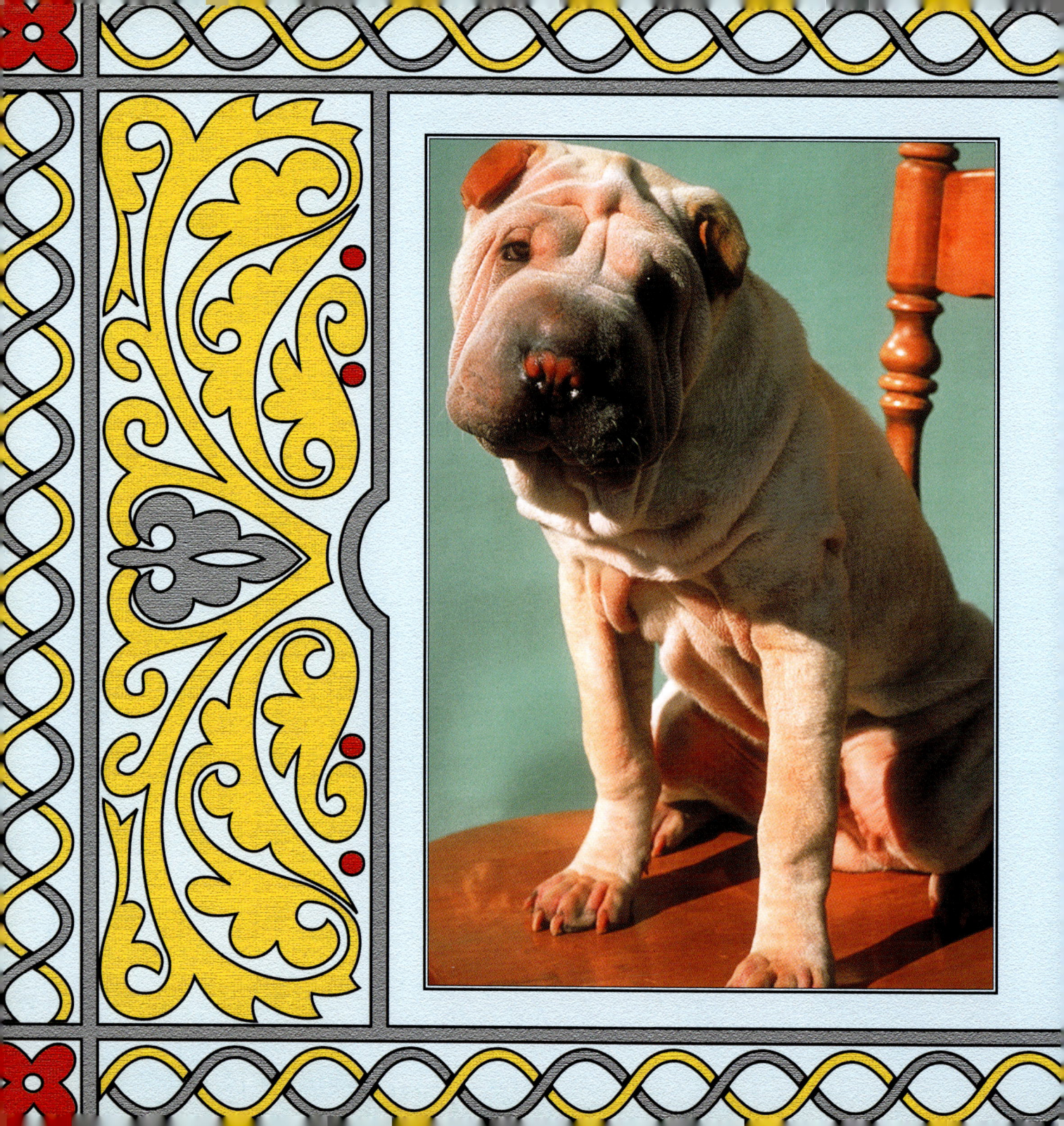

Amusing Stories

So you can't or won't recite a poem or sing a song! Telling a funny story may be easier because you can say it in your own words.

Choose one that makes you laugh. Become really familiar with it and then exaggerate and embellish as much as you like while building up to the punch line. Take your time telling it, and perhaps even put on a bit of an accent where appropriate.

Always remember the punch line.

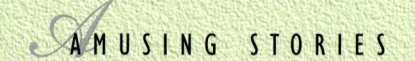

Big Chief Forget-me-Not

An Australian travel writer at the beginning of a 6-month tour of Canada was checking out of the Vancouver Hilton, and as he paid his bill, said to the manager "By the way, what's with the indian chief sitting in the lobby? He's been there ever since I arrived"

"Oh thats 'Big Chief Forget-me Not'," said the manager "The hotel is built on an indian reservation and part of the agreement is to allow the chief free use of the premises for the rest of his life. He is known as 'Big Chief Forget-me-Not' because of his phenomenal memory. He is 92 and can remember the slightest detail of his life".

The travel writer took this in, and as he was waiting for his cab, decided to put the chief's memory to the test.

"ello, mate!" said the Aussie, receiving only a slight nod in return. "What did you have for breakfast on your 21st birthday?"

"Eggs" was the chief's instant reply, without even looking up, and indeed the Aussie was impressed.

He went off on his travel writing itinerary right across to the east coast and back, telling others of Big Chief Forget-me-Not's great memory. (One local noted to him that 'How' was a more appropriate greeting for an indian chief than "ello mate".) On his return to the Vancouver Hilton six months later he was surprised to see 'Big Chief Forget-me-Not' still sitting in the lobby, fully occupied with whittling away on a stick.

"How?" said the Aussie to the Chief, who again did not stop to look up.

"Scrambled" said the Chief.

Mummy's Tummy

A little girl wandered into the bathroom whilst her mother was taking a bath and said,
"Mummy - why is your tummy so big?"
"Well, you see," said her mother,
"Daddy has given me a baby."
Downstairs later on, the little girl said to her father,
"Daddy, did you give Mummy a little baby?"
"Yes I did," said Daddy smiling.
"Well," said the little girl, *"I think she's eaten it!"*

PARTY PIECES   AMUSING STORIES

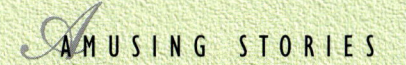

First Aid Course

At a coffee morning last week one of the ladies was enthusing about the recent First Aid course she had attended. "It was a lucky thing I went on that course," she said. "I was coming down the road yesterday when I heard a big crash behind me. I looked round and there was this poor chap who'd been knocked down by a car. He was covered in blood, and he looked to have a broken arm and compound fracture of the leg - and possibly a fractured skull. And then I remembered what I had learned on my First Aid course. So *I bent over and put my head between my legs to stop myself from fainting.*"

Eton Schoolboys

Two schoolboys at an English public school became bitter enemies. When they left school, one went into the Church and the other into the Navy. The years passed and the first boy became a Bishop, while the second attained the rank of Admiral.

One day, the bishop, now grown fat, was standing on platform six of Kings Cross station when he caught sight of his old enemy, resplendent in full admiral's uniform. "I say, porter", he said with a sly smile, "is this the right platform for Oxford?"

"It is madam," said the admiral without batting an eye, *"but do you think you should be travelling in your condition?."*

Hair-cut

Once there was a little boy who wanted his hair cut just like his Daddys - with the hole in the top for his head to come through!

Hen-Pecked Husband

There are two gates into Heaven. One has a sign saying: QUEUE HERE ALL MEN WHO ARE NOT HENPECKED BY THEIR WIVES. The other gate has a sign saying: QUEUE HERE ALL MEN WHO ARE HENPECKED BY THEIR WIVES.

Reporting for duty one morning, St. Peter saw a long line of men queuing up by the second gate, and one small, meek-looking man standing by the first gate. He asked the little man what his qualifications were for standing by the gate with the sign saying: QUEUE HERE ALL MEN WHO ARE NOT HENPECKED BY THEIR WIVES.

"I don't know really," said the man. *"My wife told me to come and queue here."*

Honey, If I Died

A wife asks her husband, "Honey, if I died, would you remarry?"

"After a considerable period of grieving, I guess I would. We all need companionship"

"If I died and you remarried," the wife asks, "would she live in this house?"

"We've spent a lot of money getting this house just the way we want it. I'm not going to get rid of my house. I guess she would."

"If I died and you remarried, and she lived in this house," the wife asks, "would she sleep in our bed?"

"Well, the bed is brand new, and it cost us $2,000. It's going to last a long time, so I guess she would."

"If I died and you remarried, and she lived in this house and slept in our bed, would she use my golf clubs?"

"Oh, no," the husband replies. *"She's left-handed"*

Pirate's Story

A pirate was talking to a "land-lubber" in a bar. The land-lubber noticed that, like any self-respecting pirate this guy had a peg leg, a hook in place of one of his hands and a patch over one eye. The land-lubber just had to find out how the pirate got in such bad shape. He asked the pirate "How did you lose your leg?" The pirate responded. "I lost my leg in a battle off the coast of Jamaica!" His new acquaintance was still curious so he asked. "What about your hand. Did you lose it at the same time?"

"No." answered the pirate. "I lost it to the sharks off the Florida Keys." Finally, the land-lubber asked, "I notice you also have an eye patch. How did you lose your eye?" The pirate answered. "I was sleeping on a beach when a seagull flew over and crapped right in my eye."

The land-lubber asked. "How could a little seagull crap make you lose your eye?" The Pirate snapped *"It was the day after I got me hook!"*

House Builder

A house builder I heard about recently was telephoned by a lady to complain about the vibrations that shook the structure of her new house when a train passed by four blocks away. "Ridiculous," he told her. "I'll be out to check it." "Just wait until the train comes along," said the lady when the builder arrived for his inspection. "Why, it nearly shakes me out of bed. Just lie down there; you'll see."

The builder scoffed but accepted her challenge. He had just stretched himself out on the bed when the woman's husband came home. "What are you doing on my wife's bed?" the husband demanded. The terrified builder shook like a leaf. "WOULD YOU BELIEVE" he said "I'M WAITING FOR A TRAIN?"

Phone-call

The maid picked up the phone and murmured something before slamming down the receiver. "Who was that Polly? I'm expecting a call".

"Only some idiot from New Zealand. He said it was a long distance from New Zealand. *I told him I knew that!"*

PARTY PIECES   AMUSING STORIES

Old Man Dying

The old man was dying and he called his wife and family to his bedside. There were four sons - three fine, big boys and a little one. He said to his wife in a weak voice, "Don't lie to me now - I want to know the truth. The little one - is he really mine?" "Oh, yes, dear," said his wife. "He really is - I give you my word of honour."

The old man smiled and slipped peacefully away. With a sigh of relief, the widow muttered, *"Thank God he didn't ask me about the other three!"*

Cats In Heaven

A little boy is gone to school one day and while he is gone, his cat gets killed. His mother is very concerned about how he will take the news. Upon his arrival home, she explains the tragedy and tries to console the boy saying, "But don't worry, the cat is in heaven with God now."

To which the boy replied, *"What's God gonna do with a dead cat?"*

Baby Priscilla

The proud young mother was discussing with her husband what they should call the new baby. "I've made up my mind," she declared firmly. "We'll call her Priscilla." The husband didn't like the name at all, but he decided to be subtle about it.

"That's a lovely name, dear," he said. "The first girl I ever went out with was called Priscilla and it will bring back pleasant memories."

"I think we'll call her Margaret, after my mother," said the wife.

Winnie the Pooh

It was the first day after Christmas vacation in a 2nd grade class. The teacher told the class that each student could tell the class one thing they got for Christmas. So the teacher calls on a girl to come up to the front of the class and tell everyone one thing she got. My daddy got me a "Bow - Wow" she said.

The teacher tells the class that they are old enough to know the correct words for things without using nicknames. The teacher tells the girl to try again. The girl thinks real hard …… "My dad got me a dog." She sat down and a boy got up and said "I got a choo-choo!" The teacher scolded him and told him to try again. The boy thought hard and said "I got an electric train!"

That boy sits down and a really shy kid gets up and sadly says, "I got a book!" The teacher feels bad for the kid and she asks "What was the title of the book?" The boy thinks hard. The class waits as the boy is thinking. Finally the boy's face brightened and he said

"Winnie the ………Shit"

The Artist

An artist celebrated for his artistic studies of the female nude arrived at the studio one morning with a terrible hangover. His model started to undress, but the artist stopped her. "Keep your clothes on, for a while," he said, "I'm not ready to start working yet; I must have some coffee and aspirins." The sympathetic model taking in at a glance his unhappy state, generously offered to make the coffee for him, which offer the artist accepted with relief.

The coffee having been made, the two were just sitting down to drink it, when familiar footsteps were heard ascending the staircase. The artist leaped to his feet. "Goodness," he exclaimed "That's my wife. She mustn't see us like this. *Quick Miss Smith, get your clothes off.*"

Memento

"Do you have any mementos in your locket, Mrs. Murphy?"
"A lock of my husbands hair".
"But he's still alive".
"Yes but his hair is all gone"!

We Survived!

We are survivors - all of us who were born before 1945. Consider the changes we have witnessed:-

We were born before television, before penicillin, before polio shots, frozen foods, Xerox, contact lens, Frisbees and the PILL.

We were before radar, credit cards, split atoms, laser beams and ball-point pens; before panty hose, dishwashers, clothes dryers, electric blankets, air conditioners, and before man walked on the moon.

We got married first and THEN lived together. How quaint and different can you be? In our time, closets were for clothes, not for "coming out of". Bunnies were small rabbits and beetles were not Volkswagens.

We were before house-husbands, gay rights, computer dating, dual careers, and computer marriages. We were before day-care centres, group therapy and nursing homes. We never heard of FM radio, tape decks, electric typewriters, C.D's, artificial hearts, word processors, yogurt and guys wearing earrings. For us time sharing meant togetherness ... a "chip" meant a piece of wood; hardware meant Hard Wear. and software wasn't even a word.

In 1940 "Made in Japan" meant JUNK. Pizzas, "MacDonalds", and instant coffee were unheard of.

In our day cigarette smoking was fashionable, GRASS was mowed, COKE was a cold drink, and POT was something you cooked in. Rock Music was a Grandma's lullaby and AIDS were helpers.

We were certainly not before the difference between the sexes was discovered, but we were surely before the sex change. We made do with what we had! And we were the last generation that was so dumb as to think that you needed a husband to have a baby!

No wonder we are so confused and there is such a generation gap today. But we *survived!*

Party Pieces   *Amusing Stories*

Golf Lesson

The new golf club member decided he knew it all. He declined the services of the professional, and made his lordly way out on to the course. He teed up, drove mightily and the ball skimmed away over the hedge and onto the main road. A few moments later, the professional dashed up. "Did you hit that ball over the hedge just now?" he asked. The clever one nodded. "Well," said the professional. "You may be interested to know that the ball hit a passing cyclist, knocking him off his bicycle, a bus which was following had to swerve to avoid running over the cyclist and as a result knocked down the wall of a cottage on the corner of the road. There are now three break-down lorries, two squad cars with policemen, four Ambulance men, one doctor, and a traffic jam of two miles long in each direction."

"Goodness" said the smart golfer, paling visibly and his confidence evaporating rapidly. "What shall I do?" The professional seized his opportunity. *"Hold the club, so,"* he instructed. *"Now, watch your stance, head down ..."*

Banker In Love

A prominent City banker fell in love with an actress and for several weeks, he took her out and about to all the fashionable nightclubs and restaurants. Deciding to ask her to marry him, he prudently engaged a firm of private detectives to check her relations and friends, since any hint of scandal might jeopardise his position in the City.

In due course he received their report: Miss Robinson appears to have led a blameless existence, and there are no indications of promiscuity, drugs, or criminal activities. Her friends and acquaintances are similarly beyond reproach. The only thing we have been able to discover about her is that in recent weeks, she has been seen around in the company of a *City banker of doubtful reputation!*

The beggar

A poor beggar shuffled over, holding out his hand. "Please give a poor blind man a pound, Sir".

"But you can see out of one eye".

"Then make it 50p."!

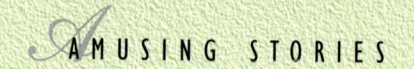

Going To A Party

A young man rang up a friend of his to invite him to a party. "You know the address, don't you?" he said. "You can't miss it - when you get to the town hall, take the third turning on the right, and we're the fifth house along. Just ring the bell with your elbow."

"Why my elbow?" said his friend.

"Well you're not coming empty-handed are you?" he said.

George Bernard Shaw

George Bernard Shaw once sent Winston Churchill two tickets for the first night of one of his plays. Attached to the tickets was a note: *Bring a friend - if you have one.*

Churchill was busy that evening, so he returned the tickets to Shaw with a note which read: Can't make tonight. *I'll come to the second performance - if there is one.*

Las Vegas

A fellow visited Las Vegas and lost all his money at the tables. He didn't even have enough money left to go to the toilet and he was obliged to borrow a coin from another patron of the gaming rooms. When he got to the toilets, however, another fellow was just coming out of one of the cubicles. Holding the door open, this fellow said, "Here you are - use this one."

Returning to the tables afterwards, our hero used the coin to play a slot machine - and won. With his winnings, he went back to the roulette table and by the end of the evening he had won a huge amount of money.

Rich and famous he went round the country lecturing on his experiences, and declaring that if he ever met his benefactor, he would split his winnings with him. In one audience, a man at the back of the hall jumped up and shouted, "I'm the man who gave you the coin!"

"You're not the one I'm looking for," said the lucky winner. *"I'm looking for the man who left the door open!"*

PARTY PIECES   AMUSING STORIES

In a Foreign Land

There was a student named Donald MacDonald from the Isle of Skye, who was admitted to Oxford University, and was now living in the hall of residence in his first year there.
His clan was very excited that one of their own was attending such a prestigious university but were concerned how he'd do in "that strange land". After the first month, his mother came to visit (no doubt carrying reinforcements of whisky and oatmeal.)
"And how do you find the English students, Donald?" she asked.

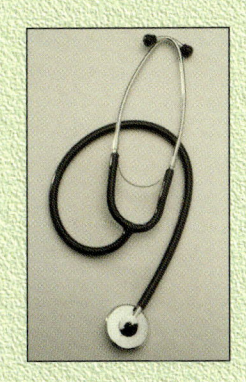

"Mother," he replied in his thick brogue. "They're such terrible noisy people. The one on that side keeps banging his head against the wall and won't stop. The one on the other side screams and screams, away into the night."
"Oh Donald! How do you manage to put up with these awful noisy English Neighbours?"

"Mother, I do nothing. I just ignore them. *I just stay here quietly, playing my bagpipes ..."*

Doctor's Reception

A man was waiting in a doctor's reception room when a young girl came out of the surgery sobbing bitterly. "What's the matter?" he asked sympathetically "The doctor's just told me I'm pregnant," she said.

It was the man's turn next and when he went into the doctor's surgery, he said, "Is that young lady really pregnant?" "No", said the doctor, *"but it's cured her hiccups."*

The Fight

Walking into the bar, Jimmy said to the bartender, "Pour me a stiff one, Albert. I just had another fight with the little woman."

"Oh yeah", said Albert. "And how did this one end?"

"When it was over," Jimmy replied, "she came to me on her hands and knees."

"Really? Now that's a switch! What did she say?"

She said, *"Come out from under the bed, you gutless weasel!"*

Party Pieces   Amusing Stories

Rodeo Champion

A Washington sports reporter was interviewing the sixty-year-old rodeo champion in Austin, Texas. The newspaperman remarked, "You're really an extraordinary man to be a rodeo champion at your age."

"Shucks," said the cowboy, "I'm not nearly the man my pa is. He's still place - kicking for a football team and he's eighty-five." "Amazing!" gasped the journalist. "I'd like to meet your father." "Can't right now. He's in El Paso standing up for Grandpa. Grandpa is getting married tomorrow. He's a hundred and thirteen."

"Your family is simply unbelievable," said the newspaperman. "Here you are, a rodeo champion at sixty. Your father's a football player at eighty-five. And now your grandfather wants to get married at a hundred and thirteen."

"Hell, mister, you got that wrong," said the Texan. "GRANDPA DOESN'T *WANT* TO GET MARRIED. HE *HAS* TO."

New Route for Train

When the railway company was planning its new route from Dublin to the coast, they wrote to a farmer advising him that the proposed line would run right through the middle of his barn. They offered him very good compensation amounting to ten times as much as the property was worth, so it came as something of a shock to his wife when he turned the offer down. 'It's a good offer' she exclaimed 'Why don't you take it?'

'No!' he said. *Do you think I'm going to keep running out to that barn day and night to open and shut the door every time they want to run a train through it?'*

Doctor/Patient

The doctor was puzzled. Eddie had come for a check up and nothing seemed wrong. "I'm very sorry but I can't diagnose your trouble, Eddie. I think it must be the drink".

"Don't worry about it, Doctor. I'll come back when you're sober."

Visiting The Pope

A friend of mine of Italian ancestry had one dream: that was to go to Italy and see the Pope. He saved his money up and finally had enough to make the trip. Just before he was about to leave, my friend went to the barbershop to get his hair cut, and the barber asked, "How are you going to get to Italy?" "I'm taking Culture Airlines." The barber said, "Forget it. They've got a terrible reputation; you'll be sorry. Where are you gonna stay?" He said, "I am gonnna stay at the Robinson in Rome." The barber said "Forget it. They give terrible service. What are you going to do when you're there in Rome?" My friend answered, "I'm gonna see the Pope." "You'll never see the Pope," the barber said. "You're a nobody, you're a Mister Zero. The Pope only sees important people. Forget it!"

Well, about five weeks later the same man went back to the barbershop. The barber said, "So you never got to Italy." My friend replied, "Yes I did. I flew Culture Airlines and they were just wonderful to me. When I got to Rome I stayed at the Robinson and they treated me like a king." The barber asked, "What did you do when you got there?" "I went to see the Pope."

"Well what happened?" asked the barber anxiously. "Well I bent down and kissed the Pope's ring." "Wow, you kissed the Pope's ring! What did he say?" "Well the Pope looked down at me and said, 'SON, WHERE DID YOU GET THAT TERRIBLE HAIRCUT?'"

Two Irish Astronauts

Two Irish astronauts landed on the moon and one of them left the spaceship to take a walk round the lunar landscape, leaving the other one to prepare for the journey home. After about an hour, there was a knock on the door of the spaceship. The second astronaut looked up and said, *"Who's there?"*